CHANGE YOUR ENERGY

CHANGE YOUR ENERGY

HEALING CRYSTALS FOR HEALTH, WEALTH, LOVE & LUCK

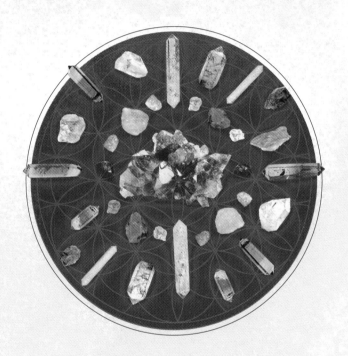

krista n. mitchell

STERLING ETHOS

New York

STERLING ETHOS
New York

An Imprint of Sterling Publishing Co., Inc.
1166 Avenue of the Americas
New York, NY 10036

Text © 2016 by Krista N. Mitchell

This publication includes alternative therapies and is intended for informational purposes only.
The publisher does not claim that this publication shall provide or guarantee any benefits,
healing, cure, or any results in any respect. This publication is not intended to provide or replace
conventional medical advice, treatment, or diagnosis or be a substitute to consulting with
a physician or other licensed medical or health-care provider. The publisher shall not be liable
or responsible in any respect for any use or application of any content contained in this publication
or any adverse effects, consequence, loss, or damage of any type resulting or arising from,
directly or indirectly, the use or application of any content contained in this publication. Any
trademarks are the property of their respective owners, are used for editorial purposes only,
and the publisher makes no claim of ownership and shall acquire no right, title,
or interest in such trademarks by virtue of this publication.

ISBN 978-1-4549-1932-2

Distributed in Canada by Sterling Publishing Co., Inc.
c/o Canadian Manda Group, 664 Annette Street
Toronto, Ontario, Canada M6S 2C8
Distributed in the United Kingdom by GMC Distribution Services
Castle Place, 166 High Street, Lewes, East Sussex, England BN7 1XU
Distributed in Australia by Capricorn Link (Australia) Pty. Ltd.
P.O. Box 704, Windsor, NSW 2756, Australia

For information about custom editions, special sales,
and premium and corporate purchases,
please contact Sterling Special Sales at 800-805-5489
or specialsales@sterlingpublishing.com.

Manufactured in Canada

4 6 8 10 9 7 5

www.sterlingpublishing.com

Cover photo: © Shutterstock (crystals)

CONTENTS

Introduction

ET ME START BY SAYING that I have always loved crystals! In my teens I loved their varying shapes and colors, I loved that they came from nature and that they were said to have mystical properties—to me that was just so magical! I started on the spiritual path in my late teens, when I first worked with crystals for their energy in pagan rituals and magical practices. I admit that, at the time, I didn't fully believe in them or even understand how they worked, but I felt drawn to them, so I continued to use them in my spiritual work.

I moved to New York City from Toronto in 2002 to pursue classical acting studies. At the time I was on antidepressants, but given my limited access to health care and affordable prescriptions, I decided to go off my medication and manage my anxiety and depression in more natural ways. Vigorous exercise, clubbing, and frequent "pig-out" nights, where I would binge on food all became ways that I would self-medicate my imbalances. When I would go through a particularly dark or rough patch, I would grab hold of an apache tear crystal (a translucent form of obsidian) and I would carry it around with me, rubbing it between my fingers when I needed extra comforting. This was when I began to use crystals for their healing energy.

I lost my passion for acting after a while and got caught up in the New York City bar and club scene. I was a bit of a lost soul at that time, working day after day, partying night after night, going from one relationship to the next, all the while trying to figure out what I wanted to do. A friend of mine had referred me to a psychic healer and I started to see her regularly, hoping that the energy healing and guidance I received would help me straighten out my life and help me find my way. I started feeling a calling to do that work myself, but I kept denying it because I felt unworthy of it, and also because I was afraid to take the risk. I finally confessed my yearning to my healer, and she said to me, "I've been waiting to hear you say that, because I believe you've got a gift." I started training in reiki (a hands-on Japanese energy balancing technique), and voraciously reading spiritual texts, but I was still heading down the wrong road in terms of my lifestyle choices, so the Universe finally decided to intervene and kick my butt.

When I turned thirty, my life fell apart. I hit an emotional and financial rock bottom, but I was determined to clean up the mess that had become my life. It was a tough, tough time for me. I found a job, but I wasn't making enough money to pay all my bills. I was desperately lost and unhappy, and I was struggling to manage my pain, misery, stress, and anxiety in a way that was healthy. I began offering reiki sessions as a side job, but I never expected to be doing spiritual healing full time. I didn't think such a thing was even possible.

Then I experienced a complete and total game-changer. A friend who was studying crystal therapy asked to practice some healing sessions on me in exchange for reiki sessions and I agreed. I was blown away by the effect the crystals had on me. There were times when I felt calm and serene after our sessions and other times when I experienced tremendous emotional release and felt despondent for days. But overall I felt that something was finally working in terms of shifting the pain, shame, fear, and doubt I was consistently feeling.

I began experimenting with crystal healing on my own, and then began integrating crystals into my reiki healing practice. While I loved reiki, there was something about the specificity of the work with crystals, and their pure, potent energy that resonated both for myself and for the clients who were coming to see me. Eventually, the crystals took over my healing work and pretty much every aspect of my life. I had become so passionate about working with them, sharing my experiences with them, and making them a consistent part of my own daily healing and spiritual practice, that a friend referred to me one day as the "Rock Whisperer," and the title stuck.

My part-time healing work morphed into a full-time, successful professional healing practice in New York City. I was offering private sessions to clients during the week and teaching on occasional weekends. Although it was a lot of work, and at times very stressful and challenging for me, I can truly say I was living my dream. I'm supremely grateful to the friend who, early on in my career, suggested that I document all my work, because much of that material is now in this book.

For years now, people have been asking me to write a book based on my work and my experience with the stones. If I had a dollar for every person who has said to me that she loved crystals but didn't know how to work with them, and then asked me if I was either teaching somewhere or if I'd written a book, I could comfortably retire! This book is entirely based on over ten years of my personal and professional healing work with crystals; it's not channeled material or stuff I read somewhere on the Internet. This is all based on working with real people with real problems, who experienced real results in their lives with crystal energy.

I've always wanted to write a book on crystals that would appeal to people regardless of their level of experience with crystals or their exposure to spiritual philosophies and practices. I believe that crystals can help anyone who chooses to work with them, no matter what their faith, background, or beliefs. This is the book!

May this work be as much of a blessing to you as it has been to me, and to the countless people whom crystals have touched and transformed throughout their lives!

Blessings to you,
"Rock Whisperer" Krista N. Mitchell

How To Use This Book

THIS BOOK IS MEANT TO BE a practical handbook on how to work with crystals, as well as a reference book for more seasoned users. If you are new to crystals, I encourage you to read the whole "Basics" section before diving in, as this can help you approach the work in the most safe, effective, and practical way. All suggestions in this book are user-friendly and tested by experience. I've learned that if things aren't practical, people won't try them, and if they're not effective, they won't try them again! All this work is based on my years of working with crystals both personally and as a full-time professional spiritual healer, teacher, and consultant in New York City. All case studies and anecdotes have had names and details altered to protect my clients' privacy, but all crystal suggestions and their results are consistent.

There are six different methods I share for working with crystals: as combinations (a group of two crystals or more) to be worn on your body, as crystal tonics (water that you imbue with crystal energy and then imbibe), as combinations to be used in the bath, pairings to hold while relaxing or meditating, as combinations whose energy is to be absorbed while sleeping, and as crystal healing layouts (the placement of crystals on the body in specific patterns to promote healing). The "Healing Crystals for Your Life" section provides crystal combinations that can be worn on a daily basis, used while you sleep, while you're meditating, or as otherwise indicated. How you work with crystals is limited only by your imagination, but I have found these six methods to be the most practical and effective. The "Do-It-Yourself Crystal Healing" section teaches you safe techniques for crystal bath, layout, and tonic work, as they have specific requirements.

An important note: There are nearly one hundred crystals and stones mentioned in this book, which are identified by image and description in the Crystal Appendix, in the insert that follows page 224. To date, there are hundreds of known or identified crystals, rocks, and stones on this Earth. I have chosen the ones in this book for their versatility, potency, capability, availability, and affordability. However, if you feel drawn to substitute one for another not mentioned in this book, honor your intuition and go for it! I make one exception to this rule: When making crystal tonics, or placing crystals in your bathwater, thoroughly research any substitutes you plan to make in advance, as many crystals can be toxic. If you're in doubt, do without.

part 1

THE BASICS

CHAPTER

1

What Are Crystals and How Do They Work?

N GEOLOGICAL TERMS, A CRYSTAL IS A MINERAL, a naturally occurring, inorganic substance characterized by a specific crystalline structure. Its chemical composition is determined by the combination, or singularity, of the known chemical elements. All crystals are arranged into groups, based on their chemical composition and crystalline structure. Currently, there are about three thousand different types of known minerals, which make up the building blocks of all the rocks on Earth.

Crystals and stones are formed by magma, or gases, in the Earth's core; volcanic lava streams; the salt beds of lakes, rivers, and oceans; as well as from the sedimentation process. The mineral and/or organic material present in either a crystal or a stone can affect its use and the quality of its energy. For example, clear quartz crystal is pure silicon oxide, which is a general amplifier and magnifier of energy. However, when it combines with colloidal iron hydrates, it becomes citrine, with a different color and energetic properties, like attracting wealth, optimism, and vitality. This is how we get crystals in the same family, like quartz or calcite, that have different colors, energy, and uses.

Crystals have been used since ancient times in healing, ritual, and magical practices. In modern times they are everywhere: They are found in the microchips of computers, ultrasound devices, lasers, watches, and other forms of electronic equipment. Some people collect them as decorative objects; others grind them up and incorporate them into holistic treatments or cosmetic products; still others use them in geomantic arts, like the Chinese system of feng shui, which is designed to impact, improve, or alter the flow of energy in a space.

HOW DO CRYSTALS WORK?

Atoms group together to form the essential shapes and qualities of crystals and stones. The particles of these atoms (protons, neutrons, and electrons) are basic units of energy that emit subtle vibrations. Because each crystal and stone has its own unique molecular and geometric structure, their vibrations resonate on differing frequencies, which are then felt and/or perceived by us as feelings and qualities.

As human beings we each have our own atomic, molecular, and energetic structure, which causes each of us to vibrate at differing frequencies, just like crystals. Our health, feelings, thoughts, and beliefs affect our vibration and vice versa. So, for instance, if we're stressed, we're vibrating at a lower frequency, which can then lead to illness or attract unfortunate circumstances into our lives. If we're happy, we're vibrating at a higher frequency, which promotes healing and can attract fortunate circumstances. It's all interrelated. With crystal healing, the singular or combined vibration of different crystals and stones affects our own vibration, so that we can positively impact our overall health and well-being, and change the circumstances we attract into our lives.

When we are in close proximity to a given crystal or crystal combination, its energy affects our own. Just as food that is exposed to microwaves gets hot, or the full moon moves the tides, crystal energy affects our whole system, meaning our physical, mental, emotional, and spiritual selves. The great thing about this is that while we can work on specific issues with a crystal, we can also address more than one issue simultaneously. Take note that this also means that, while you may be working with a crystal for one specific reason, it may be affecting you in other ways that may or may not be desirable. This is why it's important to know what you're working with before you begin.

Crystals are nondual, meaning that they do not distinguish between right and wrong, good and bad, dark and light—the classifications by which we have organized and categorized our world and our experiences. This is important to note, because you can do harm to yourself or others with crystals. Clear quartz can cause a tumor to grow, blue tiger eye can diminish the libido, lithium or rose quartz can decrease a person's sense of ambition. A crystal's effects may need to be balanced or influenced by another crystal, or avoided altogether, depending on the results you want.

I tell my students that there are as many ways of working with crystals as there are people working with them: It's a highly subjective and intimate healing art. I work with crystals in four primary ways: to absorb lower or harmful energy, to dissolve or release blockages, to provide the energy we need to heal and transform our lives, and to increase the flow of chi through the body. (Chi is the natural life force or essence that animates and flows through all life forms. It is also known by other names, such as qi, prana, mana, and ether.)

COMBINING CRYSTALS

You can work with a single crystal on its own, or you can put together a combination of crystals to achieve a desired result. I love to cook, and I was naturally drawn to combining crystals, just as you would mix ingredients in a recipe. This really opens up possibilities, because just a few crystals grouped into different combinations can address a wider range of issues. You can work with citrine for optimism, and green aventurine for self-love, but paired together they can also help you feel more awake and alert midafternoon, or recover from a respiratory illness more quickly. If you add in sunstone for confidence, and red jasper for grounding, you've now got a powerful combination that will help empower you in honoring and affirming your boundaries. You'll still have the influence of each crystal's individual properties, but then you'll also have the benefits of their combined energy.

I'm often asked if there are crystal combinations that should be avoided, and while there's no hard-and-fast rule on this, I encourage people to use common sense in terms of their needs. If you're working with hematite because you need grounding, pairing it with a high-vibration stone like selenite would be counterproductive. On the other hand, certain crystal combinations can reliably produce results that you desire in all aspects of your life, which is an underlying theme of this book. For example, if you're working with selenite to elevate and enhance your meditation experience, pairing it with smoky quartz will help balance selenite's high vibration so that you can remain present and mindful in your body. Again, it's all about your needs and the results you want to achieve.

CHAPTER

Tips for Getting Started

F YOU'RE NEW TO THE WORLD OF CRYSTALS, the whole thing may seem overwhelming. The two most common questions I'm asked are where to find them and how to choose the right one. With a myriad of crystal options available and a lot of conflicting information online, it's best to be grounded in the basics before you start.

WHERE TO GET CRYSTALS

There are many places to buy or find crystals. The two most common places to find crystals are at local metaphysical shops or through an online retailer. But you can also find them in stores offering eclectic and ethnic-inspired clothing, in vintage and antique shops, at flea markets, through street vendors, or in home décor stores. I've even found them in the gift shops of several airports! If you're buying online, it's important to first check the site's refund policy so that if you don't resonate with your crystal, or you question its authenticity (unfortunately, there are many fake, synthetic, or altered crystals on the market), or you simply aren't happy with it, you can return it for a full refund. I also find it's helpful to research who owns and operates the shop: If shop owners work with crystals for healing or mine the crystals themselves, they're far more likely to be legitimate.

Always trust your intuition when buying crystals. You may wander into a shop looking for rose quartz but then feel drawn to rhodochrosite, or find that one piece of amethyst feels better when you hold it than another piece. Remember that we all vibrate on different frequencies, and our vibrations can change, so you may harmonize with one crystal better than someone else does, and you may feel drawn to one particular crystal one day, and then a different one the next. Crystals speak to us through our intuition and our senses, so as long as you're willing to trust what you're feeling or what you're feeling drawn to, you'll almost always find that you've picked the right one.

CLEARING YOUR CRYSTALS

It's very important to clear your crystals before you start working with them so that they're free from any energetic residue. Think of a spoon in a restaurant and how many times it's used by different people throughout the week—you're going to want that thing 100 percent clean before you dip it into your soup! With a few exceptions, crystals undergo a transfer of energy (usually referred to as "absorbing energy" or "transference") whenever they're exposed to new people or changing environments. This is not to say that all transference is necessarily a bad thing. I've used quartz crystals to absorb powerful healing energy from spiritual meccas like the Boynton Canyon Vortex in Sedona, Arizona, and I had a friend bring one for me to Machu Picchu during the much-prophesied spiritual ascension phase of the winter solstice of 2012. I've subsequently worked with that vortex energy to raise my vibration when I'm feeling down or tired, and the energy from Machu Picchu for greater spiritual awakening and expansion. In most cases, though, unless you know a crystal's energy is pure, it's best to always clear it before you expose yourself to its energy.

When you come in contact with a crystal, you naturally begin to attune to its energy. This essentially means that your system is familiarizing itself with the crystal's energy and its feel, and then allowing its vibration to fuse with your own. It's like first tasting a bowl of soup to sense its temperature and sample its taste before ingesting it. Now, if there's E. coli in that soup, you're going to become unwell. If you shared that soup with a friend, he's also going to become unwell. If you attune to a crystal that's been in contact with some harmful energy, you're going to be taking that into your system. And if you wear a crystal while you're angry or sick or depressed, and then pass that crystal on to another person, she'll be taking on some of that energy you left behind.

When I worked in a popular spiritual bookshop in New York, I saw all kinds of people walk in, do all sorts of things with the crystals there (including smelling them, rubbing them in strange places, and falling asleep while holding them), then leave them there for the next unsuspecting person. To this day, even if it's a crystal pulled straight from the Earth or given to me by a dear friend, I never, ever, work with that crystal until I've cleared it! This doesn't mean that you can't hold or touch a crystal briefly. It just means that it's a good idea to avoid working or coming in contact with its energy for a lengthier period until you've cleared it. Below are some methods for clearing your crystals. Choose whichever one is most practical for you:

- Pass them through the smoke of burning sage, copal, palo santo, or whichever natural element is sacred to your land a few times each per crystal.

- Place them in direct full moonlight for a night, or in direct sunlight for a maximum of 5–15 minutes. (Note: Sunlight can fade the color of certain crystals, or deplete a crystal's energy if it's exposed for too long, so I typically do not recommend using sunlight.)

- Use reiki or other healing modalities by holding the crystals in both your hands and channeling energy through them.

- Expose them for several minutes to sound vibration, using a singing bowl, Tibetan tingshas or bells, tuning forks, or the sound of your own voice as you sing a hymn or chant a sacred mantra.

- Place them in a bowl of lightly sea-salted or ocean water. (*Note:* Some crystals can become damaged when placed in water. See "Practical Crystal Uses and Tips" on page 42 for a list.) Rinse them in plain water and then let them air-dry.

- Place crystals on top of a flat piece of selenite, amethyst, or clear quartz for a minimum of 2–4 hours.

- Bury crystals in fresh soil or in uncooked organic brown rice for approximately 12 hours. (*Note:* When you're done with the rice, compost it or scatter it in a field.)

- You can use incense to clear crystals—but only if it is a high-grade, high-quality incense, made from a plant essence that has clearing properties, like sage, rue, frankincense, or myrrh. Otherwise, you're literally just blowing smoke and fragrance at your stones.

- Remember: Good crystal care also involves your jewelry! To clear the energy of crystal jewelry (both beads and in settings), you can use several of the methods above, or you can place them in the freezer overnight.

How often you need to clear your crystals depends on how often you've been working with them and for how long. The more you become in tune with the energy of your crystals, the more you'll cultivate an awareness of when they need to be cleared. Here are some general guidelines:

- Clear crystals daily if you're wearing them all day or sleeping with them at night.

- Clear weekly when you're meditating with them regularly, wearing them for shorter periods, or if you have them in your workplace or car (or other high-stress zones).

- Clear monthly if you're using the crystals to influence the flow of energy in your home, or if you're only using them once in a while.

- If you have crystals in a harmonious garden space, by broad, leafy plants, or in places of positive chi (like by a gently rolling stream or cluster of trees), there's no need to clear them because their energy is being cleared and maintained by nature.

CHARGING YOUR CRYSTALS

Just like batteries, plants, or people, crystals can get dull and tired when they're being used a lot and aren't getting time and energy to recharge. When they become drained of energy, they're no longer effective; it's like trying to drive your car on empty. I see this especially with crystals that don't need to be cleared (see "Practical Crystal Uses and Tips" on page

42 for a list), like citrine or kyanite. People assume that if they don't need to be cleared, they don't need to be charged, either, or they simply forget to do it. There are a lot of tired little citrines and kyanites rolling around out there! Though crystals are considered to be inanimate, I believe they have a life essence and consciousness, so they need to be treated with respect and care.

When a crystal needs to be charged, it can feel dull, lifeless, or less effective when you're using it. You can cultivate a greater awareness of a crystal's charge by holding it first before working with it and sensing how it feels, then comparing that sensation later on by holding it again and making a note of any difference. Through time and practice you'll be able to tell very quickly if your crystal needs to be charged.

You may notice that the charging techniques listed below are similar to, or the same as, many clearing techniques. This is because when you bring a crystal's essence back into its cleared and natural state, it's able to absorb the energy vibrations that emanate from the Earth. Human beings experience this, too, which is one of the reasons that spending time in nature or in green places can be so healing and restorative for us. Use whichever method is easiest and most practical for you, and remember that a crystal needs to be cleared before it's charged or the charging process will take longer.

- Place your crystals in a bowl and put them outside during a rainstorm. Despite the pollutants in our rainwater, its ionic charge replenishes crystals very quickly. Leave them in the collected rainwater for a few hours, then rinse them in plain water and let them air-dry.

- Place them in a bowl of ocean water, then rinse them in plain water and let them air-dry. (*Note:* I've lost a few good crystals when I've either accidentally dropped them or lost my hold on them while running them through the currents of strong ocean waves. It's preferable to collect a bowl of ocean water and use that instead.)

- Charge them by holding them in your dominant hand and channeling some form of healing energy into them for 5–10 minutes (for instance, using reiki, prana, or the like).

- Expose them for several minutes to the sound vibration of a singing bowl, Tibetan tingshas or bells, tuning forks, or the sound of your own voice as you sing a hymn or chant a sacred mantra. If you are also using this method to clear your crystals, spot-check them frequently by holding them in your receptive hand (your nondominant hand) to sense if they are first cleared, then to sense when they feel fully charged by this method.

- Put them on selenite, clear quartz, or rocks in your garden for a minimum of 2–4 hours.

- Leave them in direct, full moonlight for a night, or in direct sunlight for 5–15 minutes. (*Note:* Sunlight can fade the color of certain crystals, and/or damage a crystal's energy if it's exposed for too long.) It's best to place them outside rather than behind a window, as the replenishing part of the energy can be filtered by the glass. If this isn't possible, then I recommend choosing another method.

- Bury crystals in fresh soil or place them beside plants or in a garden for 6–12 hours. Chi collects in natural places where there's gentle movement, so you can also place them by a running stream or trees for the same amount of time.

- Shake the crystals vigorously in your hand for a minute. (*Note:* This will only do in a pinch because it won't charge them fully, so you'll still need to give them a proper charge later using one of the methods above.)

When or how often you'll need to charge your crystals will depend on how much and how often you use them. The more you become in tune with your crystals, the more you'll be able to tell when they've become depleted. Typically, they'll feel dull to you, have less of a sparkle or zing when you hold them, or you'll notice that you're not experiencing their usual effects. Trust your intuition and, if in doubt, charge them. But I'll give you some general guidelines for the intervals between charging, just in case:

- Charge weekly when you're working with crystals daily, sleeping with them at night, using them in your bathwater, or using them to make a crystal tonic.

- Charge monthly when you're working with crystals regularly for shorter periods, or if they're in your workplace or car (or other high-stress areas).

- Charge every 3–6 months if you're using your crystals to influence the flow of energy in your home, or if you only use them once in a while.

- If you have crystals in a harmonious garden space, by broad, leafy plants, or in places of positive chi (like by a cluster of trees), there's no need to charge them because their energy is being charged and maintained by nature.

If crystals are left on their own to rest for a while, they'll recharge naturally. This can take as long as a few months, depending on how much and how often they were used and whether or not they were cleared first.

STORING YOUR CRYSTALS

How you store your crystals is a matter of preference. Some people wrap them in black or red silk to help preserve their energy and keep them clear. Others keep them in boxes or on display on tabletops and shelves. You may want to keep your crystal wands separate from your tumbled stones, and place large or rough pieces in display cases.

How you want to work with your crystals can help determine where you keep them: If you're working with them as magical tools, then having them on an altar or in a place out of reach is best. When you're wearing them daily, it might be more practical to store them in a place where you can see them clearly and have quick access to them. When I'm doing healing work with clients, I find it most efficient to keep my crystals sorted by chakra in metal makeup kit boxes, and when traveling I wrap them individually and put them in soft makeup cases.

My home is a crystal explosion: I have them under pillows, by my bedside, on my desk, displayed on shelves, grouped in small bowls and seashells on tables, in the garden. . . . If it feels harmonious and pleasing to you, go for it. Follow your intuitive nudges. As an exercise, you can use your senses to test if where you've stored your crystals feels harmonious and balanced. Close your eyes, take a few deep breaths, and then stretch your awareness outside of yourself and around your crystals. Trust what you're feeling—if it feels good, then it's balanced; if it doesn't, keep experimenting.

Opinions vary when it comes to the right and wrong ways to store crystals, but if you honor your intuition and stick with what feels good to you, you'll find what works best. This is not an exact science; our relationships with crystals and their interrelationships with each other can be influenced by myriad factors.

There are a few places I don't place crystals: in windows, because the sunlight can damage them (with the exception of select stones I may use to filter incoming energy); in my drinking water, as they can be toxic and breed bacteria; near my dogs, because crystal energy can create discomfort for animals (especially small animals); or in spots where the crystals can influence another person's energy without his permission. I also keep crystals I'm working with for manifestation or with specific intentions out of other people's reach, so the crystals' energy will stay pure for my purposes. Apart from that, I'm happiest and feel healthiest when my crystals are part of my daily life as much as possible. The more you appreciate and interact with your crystals, the more they will enhance and enrich your life.

A note on crystal décor or ornamentation: Having crystals on display in your place purely for aesthetics is fine! Crystals are beautiful works of natural art. Beautiful baubles can have their own healing impact.

CHAPTER

How to
Work with Crystals

OFTEN SAY TO MY STUDENTS that there are as many ways of working with crystals as there are people working with them—you really are limited only by your imagination. That doesn't mean, however, that every way you can think of is necessarily safe, effective, or desirable. I've tried all kinds of things, including wrapping them in my hair (cute) to putting them in my socks (ouch!), to sewing some inside my underwear (let's not go there). All that being said, I've tried and tested simple ways of learning how to work with crystals, as well as practical, enjoyable, and rewarding methods of incorporating their healing energy into our daily lives.

ATTUNING TO A CRYSTAL

After clearing your crystal, it's important to take 5–10 minutes to attune to it before working with its energy. Attuning to a crystal means exposing yourself to its energy so that you can become familiar with it and your body can adjust or respond to its vibrations. You need to test it out so that you know how it feels to you, what effect it has on you, and whether its energy is beneficial or harmonious for you and your purposes. This is the best way to learn about your crystal. This way you'll always know what it does, what it's like, and how it works for you. Therefore, you'll know when it's best for you to use it.

When I'm training crystal healers, I always have them select a crystal, read about it, then attune to it and make note of their experience. It's a good idea to look up a crystal's properties first, either in a book or online, so that you have an idea of what other people have experienced in working with it. It's akin to rooting for food in the woods: It's wise to know if a plant poisoned someone before you eat it! That's a dramatic example, but crystals can have adverse effects, so it's always best to be mindful. Some crystals, like calcites, for instance, have very gentle, slow, and smooth energies that you can wear daily for subtle support. Others, like malachite, may have a very abrupt and dramatic effect on the emotions, which may make you feel like a hot mess for a while. Bear in mind that when you look into the metaphysical properties of a crystal, what you find will be based on the author's experience. What you experience could be something altogether different, so be willing to honor what you feel over what you read.

If you want to skip that step and go by intuition alone, you certainly can—just be sure to note how it makes you feel for future reference. I remember wearing pietersite one day to boost my intuition; it made me feel very moody, aggravated, and short-tempered. I came home and looked it up, and, sure enough, while it's great for boosting intuition, pietersite also has a storm element to it that stirs things up inside. I knew going forward to work with that crystal only when I was in a good, solid place.

To attune to a crystal, sit quietly and hold it in your receptive hand for 5–10 minutes. Close your eyes and take a few deep breaths to help you relax. Focus your awareness on the crystal. Feel its weight, its shape, and its texture in your hand. Notice if you feel it getting warmer, any tingling or buzzing in your hand, or any energy moving up through your arm or body. As the crystal energy flows into you, you may become aware of images, colors, sounds, words, thoughts, memories, or feelings surfacing. Just notice them and let them pass through you. Even if you feel nothing at all, your body will be familiarizing itself with the crystal's energy. Allow your process to be whatever it is, because the process is always perfect.

After attuning to your crystal, make a note of what you've experienced. People always ask me how I can remember the properties of so many crystals, and my answer is because I've experienced them. It's kind of like eating a certain food or listening to a song—you remember what it's like afterwards because you've experienced it. This is the most effective way to learn about different stones. If you start to feel any discomfort from the crystal's energy, if something feels wrong or if you feel uneasy, put it aside and contemplate what you felt and why. It might be that either the crystal's energy is not harmonious with yours and therefore was throwing you off balance, or it might be that the crystal was bringing emotions to the surface that you need to address or heal.

One of my students, Celeste, attuned to carnelian and hated it: It felt uncomfortable in her hand and stirred up feelings of anger and distrust. I asked her to contemplate whether the crystal was throwing her out of balance, or if it was bringing an internal imbalance up to her awareness. She thought about it and realized that these were feelings she had toward a classmate that she was repressing and needed to work through. Her system was having a healing response to carnelian, so it was a good crystal for her to work with (at an appropriate time), rather than something she needed to avoid.

Debbie, on the other hand, meditated with selenite and it made her feel very uncomfortable. When I asked her to contemplate the cause of her discomfort, she replied that it made her feel dizzy and out of her body. She had a lot of trouble staying grounded in her life, and the selenite was only making her worse. This was a clear indication that it was a crystal she should avoid in the future, as it was throwing her way off balance.

SIX METHODS FOR WORKING WITH CRYSTALS

In this book we focus on six principal ways of working with crystals: wearing them, bathing with them, making crystal tonics, doing crystal therapy layouts, sleeping with them, and meditating while holding them. All these methods have proven effective and reliable over my twenty years of working with crystals personally, and in my years of doing professional healing work.

1. **WEARING CRYSTALS:** When working with smaller crystals or working with crystal energy for longer periods, it's best to wear them. By wearing them, I mean on your body, either in the form of jewelry, in pockets, in your bra, in a neck pouch or medicine bag, or by holding them and carrying them around with you. When crystals are relatively small (say, less than 2½"/6.5cm in size), you need to have them in contact with your body so that they can be effective. Leaving them at home, in your purse, or in your locker doesn't work; they won't radiate sufficient energy to impact your system. Think of a lightbulb: Small bulbs emit very little light so you need to have them close by in order to be able to see. Large bulbs emit more light, so they can be farther away. I'm typically either wearing crystal jewelry or have crystals in a pouch stuffed in my bra, or both. I'm less likely to lose them or have them fall off and break when they're in a pouch, and they're also less likely to irritate my skin.

2. **BATHING WITH CRYSTALS:** The benefit of bathing with crystals is that they can energize your bathwater so that you receive greater healing impact in less time. You're literally soaking in healing crystal energy! Many people (myself included) enjoy pairing the relaxing, restorative experience of a long hot bath with the added benefit of crystal vibes. But you can also use this method to increase vitality, boost your immune system, clear your aura, and much more.

3. **CRYSTAL TONICS:** Similar to bathing with crystals, making crystal tonics involves energizing drinking water with crystal energy. While crystal tonics are more subtle and cumulative in their effects, their benefit is that they can be much more practical. Many of my clients work in fashion, television, and other forms of media, and are not able to wear crystals with their outfits, so taking a crystal tonic is an easy way for them to get a dose of healing energy throughout the day. This is also an excellent alternative for people who travel regularly, for those who don't want to meditate or don't have time to do it, or for people who don't want to buy a whole ton of crystals for healing purposes.

4. **CRYSTAL HEALING LAYOUTS:** This is the ancient art of the laying on of stones, which you can practice on yourself with ease, in the privacy of your own home, using your own crystals whenever it's desirable or convenient. It's like

having a crystal spa session: You lie down, place crystals in specific positions and combinations on your body, and then relax for 20–60 minutes. You can light candles, play soothing music, even dab on some aromatherapy oils if it strikes your fancy, and then let the crystals do their work. This is my favorite method of crystal healing because it's so deeply effective and all I have to do is lie there for a while. It's also incredibly economical once you've made your initial investment in your crystal collection! I use layouts whenever I'm feeling sick, if I'm really tired or drained, to help clear my aura, to reduce stress if I feel down, and to support my overall wellness.

5. SLEEPING WITH CRYSTALS: This sounds like it might be uncomfortable, but we spend a lot of time in bed (if we're lucky!), so it's a great time to subtly work on psychic or spiritual development, stress relief, aura clearing, staving off bad dreams or disruptive spirits, or sleeplessness. I like this method because it's also the easiest way to work crystal healing into your daily life. You can place crystals under your pillows, by your bedside, at your feet, or at the top of your head, or sleep while wearing them in a soft cloth pouch hanging around your neck. This is the best method for people who are too pressed for time to use any of the other methods mentioned in this book. Even if you're only getting a few hours of sleep at night, this method will still be effective.

6. **MEDITATING WITH CRYSTALS:** Along with the various nerve endings that make our hands sensitive, we also have chakras (spiritual energy centers located in our bodies that regulate our life forces [see "The Chakra System," page 184]) in our palms. These make sensing, emitting, and receiving energy through our hands possible. When you hold a crystal in your hand during meditation, its energy flows into your body through your palm chakra. You can use this method either in support of your meditation practice or for the purpose of energy healing. I'll hold crystals to help quiet my mind or enhance my meditation practice, but I'll also opt for specific crystals to hold while meditating if I'm feeling tired and need a boost, if I want to feel more grounded, if I'm working on self-love, or if I'm looking for greater focus and intuitive guidance that day. Multitask your meditation? Why not! These are busy times, and I'm all about getting the most bang for your buck.

CRYSTAL SIZES

The size of your crystal will determine how much energy it emits. So when deciding which size you need, it all depends on how you're planning to work with it. There are also practical considerations: If you're carrying a crystal in your pocket, it can't be the size of a baseball. Conversely, if you've placed a crystal in your room to help create a relaxing atmosphere, a crystal the size of a quarter is not going to be very effective. Again, let's consider our lightbulb analogy: Smaller bulbs emit less light, while larger bulbs emit more light.

As a general guideline, use smaller sizes (½"–2½"/13mm–6.5cm approximately) when wearing them on your body, making tonics, or doing crystal healing layouts. Use larger sizes (3"/7.5cm-plus) when bathing, sleeping, meditating, or for crystals in your home. I urge you to trust your intuition here: If something feels as if it's too big, it probably is; if it feels as if it's too small, it probably is. Give things a try and pay attention to your experience. Switch things up until you find what you feel works for you.

WHAT TO FOCUS ON FIRST

I'm fond of saying that we're all our own favorite fixer-uppers. There are always things for us to work on, heal, shift, cultivate, and grow. The amount of information, suggestions, and options in this book may definitely feel overwhelming. If you find that there's more than one thing you want to work on at a time, don't overload yourself: Choose a couple of priorities and then layer your methods. If you're already wearing citrine and amethyst as a daily crystal combination to counter depression, but you also want to attract more wealth, try adding an abundance bath, or a prosperity crystal healing layout into your weekly routine. If you're using crystal layouts to heal from heartbreak, but you also want to explore more of your spiritual side, try meditating regularly with selenite or by placing moonstone under your pillow at night.

Keep in mind that in working with crystals you can address more than one issue at a time, but you need to make sure that you're not pushing your process or overwhelming your system. Rebekah had a long list of things she was working on with crystals. She was taking love-inviting baths, she was consuming one crystal tonic for calmness and another one for intuition, she was doing a healing layout almost every day for weight

Continued on page 46

PRACTICAL CRYSTAL USES AND TIPS

- **BABY ROOMS:** Kids and babies love crystals! The sweet, soothing vibrations of blue calcite and rose quartz are excellent choices for a child's room. Just make sure they're placed well out of reach of the infant (never in the crib) and that the pieces aren't small enough for a child to swallow.

- **BALANCING HIGH VIBRATIONS:** If you find the energy of high-vibration stones (like danburite, selenite, or moldavite) overwhelming, holding or wearing smoky quartz helps you balance the energy by grounding it in your body.

- **BATHROOMS:** Placing large blue crystals and stones in the bathroom creates a calming, soothing atmosphere. If you'd prefer a more invigorating atmosphere, opt for yellow, green, or clear crystals.

- **BEDROOMS (RELATIONSHIPS):** Place pieces of rose quartz, garnet, and ruby by your bed, under your pillow, or in your love and marriage area, if you practice feng shui, to attract romantic love into your life or to keep passion in your relationship.

- **BROKEN CRYSTALS:** If your crystal breaks, hold it in your receptive hand and feel for a vibration. If you feel a buzz, you can still work with it. If it feels dull or lifeless, return it to the Earth by burying it in the ground or releasing it to the ocean.

- **CHOOSING A CRYSTAL:** You'll know if a crystal is right for you by how good it feels when you're holding it in your receptive hand.

- **CONCENTRATION AND FOCUS:** Place a sphere or a large piece of fluorite on your desk for support when studying or to help you maintain more focus at work.

- **FLOWERS:** Place any crystal near flowers to help them grow taller and last longer.

- **FOOD (CLEARING THE ENERGY OF):** Did you know that your food also absorbs emotional energy? Put a pouch with jet, green aventurine, and green calcite in your lunch bag, your fruit bowl, or with the snacks in your desk drawer to clear your food of any lower or harmful frequencies.

- **FOOD (VITALITY):** Store a large piece of quartz with your fresh produce to keep it fresh and vital for a longer time.

- **GARDENS:** You can give plants and trees a boost of crystal energy in place of toxic fertilizers. Citrine, moss agate, and clear quartz work best in this regard.

- **HOME (HARMONY):** Keep pieces of apophyllite, amethyst, and rose quartz in rooms where you want sweetness, harmony, and peace.

- **HOME (PROTECTION):** Place an amethyst geode in your main window, selenite on your windowsills, and black obsidian in all corners to help protect the energy of your home. If the situation is especially bad (a client of mine once, unfortunately, lived next

PRACTICAL CRYSTAL USES AND TIPS

to a meth lab), line the interior perimeter of your home with either selenite sticks or sea salt.

- **HOME (SANCTUARY):** Large amethyst specimens (like geodes, cathedrals, or points) help to create a soothing, comfortable, positive environment.

- **LOW-MAINTENANCE CRYSTAL METHOD:** Crystal healing doesn't have to be complicated or time-consuming. If you can't sit to meditate and don't want to wear crystals or make crystal tonics, you can try holding crystals in both hands to balance your energy while watching TV, sitting on the bus, talking on the phone, or waiting for an appointment. Rose quartz, apophyllite, smoky quartz, black tourmaline, and moonstone are all good choices.

- **OFFICE (CLEARING):** Place selenite towers (or large pieces) in the four corners of your office, cubicle, or workplace to purify the energy and increase the flow of positive chi there without having to use sacred smoke, sprays, or sounds.

- **PROSPERITY:** Pieces of citrine and pyrite placed in shop windows and cash registers can help attract more customers and boost sales. You can also place these crystals at your desk, in your workspace, or in your money area, if you practice feng shui.

- **RECEPTIVE HAND VERSUS DOMINANT:** Your receptive hand is the hand you do not write with, your dominant hand is the one you do write with, and if you're ambidextrous, you need to experiment by holding a crystal in each hand to determine which feels more receptive.

- **SPAS AND THERAPY ROOMS:** Large clusters of apophyllite help to amplify healing energy, create feelings of serenity, and welcome divine presence.

- **SUNLIGHT:** Crystals featured in this book that can fade in color if left in direct sunlight are aquamarine, azurite, celestite, colored calcites, colored quartz (citrine, amethyst, rose, etc.), fluorite, hiddenite, jade, and pink kunzite.

- **TUMBLED VERSUS ROUGH STONES:** I prefer to work with rough stones when doing layouts, making tonics, or while in meditation because I find that their vibrations are stronger and more direct. Tumbled or polished stones (with the exception of pointed or faceted crystals) tend to have softer or more subtle energy and are more comfortable to wear on a daily basis or when placed under pillows. Ultimately, it comes down to a matter of preference.

- **VISION BOARDS:** Place a quartz crystal cluster anywhere you want to amplify and magnify positive energy or intentions, including altars, in front of vision boards, or on top of written lists of goals and to-do lists.

- **WATER:** Crystals featured in this book that can be damaged by water are angelite, celestite, chrysanthemum stone, healer's gold, pyrite, scolecite, and selenite.

Continued from page 41

loss, and she was also meditating with high-vibration crystals to tap into more of her psychic abilities. On top of all of this crystal action, she was wearing a huge moldavite pendant, crystal jewelry, and crystals in her bra on a daily basis. She started having anxiety attacks, was seeing dark things out of the corner of her eye, and was having great difficulty sleeping. I had her ditch all the crystals and wear only a small piece of smoky quartz for one week. When her system had become grounded and stabilized, I suggested that she pick her two top priorities and start working on those, and then add in something else only when she was ready or as needed.

Honor your intuition and feelings. If something feels as if it's too much, then it's too much. Taking your time and allowing your process to unfold more slowly can actually be more productive. If you're doing too much and throwing yourself out of balance as a result, you're likely to end up sick. Remember that healing and transformation should always be a loving process.

CAUTIONS AND PRECAUTIONS

Like many things in nature, crystals can be a boon or a bane, depending on how you approach them. Just because something is natural doesn't automatically mean it's safe (think snake venom!), and when you use crystals improperly, you can harm your system. Among the key guidelines when working with crystals are to trust your intuition, honor the wisdom of your feelings, know what you're working with, and, if in doubt, do without.

Everything in this book has been tried and tested many times with favorable results, but what worked for one person may not necessarily work for you. Be open to experimenting and keeping notes about how you feel when you're working with a crystal and its aftereffects on your system.

Always err on the side of caution and accept that less is oftentimes more: Better to keep things simple as you start out, follow the guidelines in this book, and then build up when you feel more confident and experienced. Be mindful of the following three cautions when working with crystals:

- Crystals may be highly toxic, either to the touch or if their minerals are absorbed or ingested. Be sure to follow the methods described in this book when bathing with crystals or making crystal tonics. If you're concerned about skin sensitivity or if you're not sure if a crystal is safe, do not place it in your water.

- Crystals are nondual, meaning that they do not differentiate between good and bad, or right and wrong; they simply function in their purpose. Just as a tomato will taste like a tomato, a dog will behave like a dog, and the sun will rise and set, a crystal will emit its energy and do its thing. It's up to you to decide if you're using a crystal's energy for the right reasons, and to work with crystals in a manner that is safe and mindful.

- Clear quartz magnifies and amplifies everything—the good, the bad, and the ugly. Placing quartz on top of a tumor or a fungal infection, or wearing it when you're feeling anxious, will only exacerbate the situation. Similarly, if it's placed on a plant or a tree, it will help to make it grow, or it can be used to strengthen the power of attraction and manifestation. It functions singularly in its purpose.

part **2**

HEALING CRYSTALS FOR YOUR LIFE

CHAPTER

4

Love and Relationships

LOVE BEING IN LOVE! It's truly one of the greatest feelings in the world. Everything feels light and good and rosy. It tingles with the sensations of newness and possibility and so much to look forward to. I remember the first time I fell in love with a guy from Manchester. I hadn't even realized it until we took one of those rowboats out on the lake in Central Park for a laugh. A photographer was snapping photos to sell to couples and tourists, and when I looked at ours, my glowing face made it embarrassingly obvious that I was completely, head over heels, madly in love.

Everyone wants love, right? Crystals for love are by far the most popular stones out there. Whether it's dating, finding a relationship, healing from heartbreak, or cultivating self-love, working with crystal energy can make a huge difference in your love life. I've been through it all many times over and I've had crystals with me every step of the way. To quote a colleague of mine, "I'm still a Disney girl"; I still believe in true love, love at first sight, and that love conquers all, but I'm not a hopeless romantic anymore. After all, what set me firmly on the path of becoming a healer were my own experiences of heartbreak. But the experience of coming through all that to the other side and then back to love again has made me the powerful, compassionate, wiser woman that I am now. And sharing my experience with crystals through that time and how they helped me has helped many other people in turn.

DATING

I love being in love, but I loathe dating. Ha! Dating successfully all depends on your intention, energy, and perspective. Some people date to get lucky, others are looking for "the one," and the rest of us fall somewhere in between.

They've made several TV shows based on how challenging dating can be in New York City, and I've helped countless clients and friends cope with the pressures of dating and the impact it has on their self-esteem, their sense of personal fulfillment, and their perceived social status and success. Dating should be a fun way to get out there, meet people, and enjoy lovely dinners, but when you're lonely, have an agenda, don't feel good about yourself, or your biological clock's ticking, it's more like torture.

Corinne, a stunningly gorgeous, incredibly successful fashion magazine executive, started working with me because she was having trouble lining up a date, let alone getting a boyfriend. She wasn't really spiritual or into crystals, but she was desperate enough to try anything because she was tired of being single and doing things on her own. We talked about how she felt when she was out on a date: She felt tense, hyperaware of how she was behaving, second-guessing how she was coming across, and fearful that her strong personality was a turnoff. She was hoping that crystals could help her appear "softer" and more "feminine" so that she would, in turn, be more attractive. The truth is that crystals could and did help her, not because they magically changed who she was, but because they helped her tap into more of her beautiful traits and qualities.

When Corinne was relaxed, she was warm, witty, self-assured, and glowed from within, so I suggested she wear chrysocolla for calm and self-assurance, rose quartz for self-love and acceptance, smoky quartz to help ground her in the present moment, and carnelian to increase her feelings of warmth and sensuality. I also suggested that she ditch the agenda for a while and make dating an opportunity for her to cultivate these parts of herself while being in the presence of someone new. It took Corinne a few dates to get used to it, but she said at some point she noticed a shift and was able to relax more into her own self and feel the crystal energy. Three months later she was dating a man who appreciated her strength, valued her opinion, and loved her sense of humor.

The beautiful thing about being human is that every one of us possesses all the qualities, traits, and emotions we can perceive in the world. We have a tendency to focus exclusively on our faults and shortcomings, but everything we might admire in someone else we too possess. So if you think that you can't be more confident, passionate, cool, intelligent, funny, alluring, or desirable, I'm very pleased to say you're wrong! You can work with crystals to help you tap into every quality you admire and wish for yourself, because, deep down inside, you already have it. You can wear any of the following crystals to enhance your own inner qualities, and that can make going out on a date more fun, relaxing, and promising. If you want to work on more than one quality at a time, you can mix and match—just be sure to keep to a five-stone maximum so that you don't overwhelm your system.

CRYSTAL COMBINATIONS

AUTHENTICITY: Wear amazonite, sodalite, ruby, and rose quartz when you want to honor and allow more of your own authentic self to shine through.

CONFIDENCE: Wear citrine, sunstone, or pyrite to feel more grounded and secure.

COOL: Wear blue lace agate and chrysocolla to feel more like your confident, assured, and excellent self.

COURAGE: Wear red jasper and ruby when you want an extra dose of courage (that's not in liquid form).

FEMININE ENERGY: Wear pink opal and chrysocolla if you want to cultivate more of your feminine qualities. Add in carnelian if you want to spice them up a bit.

FLIRTING: Wear pink aventurine, carnelian, and garnet.

FUNNY: Wear aragonite star cluster and citrine when you want to let your sense of humor shine through.

GROUNDED AND PRESENT: Wear or hold hematite, smoky quartz, or onyx when you want to get out of your own head and feel more engaged in the present moment.

INSIGHTFULNESS: Wear amethyst when you want to be more intuitive, perceptive, and acute in your observations.

MASCULINE ENERGY: Wear pyrite, fire agate, and sunstone to cultivate more of your masculine qualities.

NERVOUSNESS: Wear or hold lithium quartz to soothe your nerves and keep your heart open and available.

RELAXED STATE: Wear ocean jasper, orange calcite, and rose quartz to feel more mellow.

SEXINESS: Wear carnelian, ruby, and garnet when you want to feel more sensual and alluring.

SPIRITUALITY: Wear moonstone when you want to embody more of your divine self.

WARMTH: Wear ruby and rubellite (red tourmaline) to exude more warmth, compassion, and loving vibes.

WITTINESS: Wear blue kyanite and fluorite when you want to impress someone with your repartee.

FINDING LOVE

I've had my fair share of clients who have asked me why some people can find love and form relationships so easily, while others seem to struggle. I've noticed that those who are successful in love have all these things in common: They're confident; they like themselves, know themselves, know what they need, and what makes them happy; they go after what they want; they're mindful of the vibe they're putting out there; and they believe they're worth it. They don't settle, and they don't kid themselves when something isn't working or doesn't feel right.

These are all important things to bear in mind when you're looking for love in your life. I've worked with so many men and women who want to be in a relationship—period—without considering what's best for them. What ends up happening is that they either become serial daters who can't seem to get to the next level (a committed relationship), or they end up in relationships with people who don't meet their needs, make them happy, or truly love them in the way they deserve.

Paola considered herself to be the "queen of first dates." She didn't have a problem snaring a man's attention or sparking his interest, but she had trouble keeping it. She was beginning to believe that she simply wasn't the type of girl guys liked or committed to beyond that first date. She knew this was having a negative effect on her sense of self-worth, and she was hoping that crystal healing could help her feel better and eliminate the mental block she felt she was forming. I suggested that she meditate daily for 20 minutes, holding rose quartz in both hands for more self-love, and that she wear amethyst, hematite, and rhodonite daily to help shift negative patterns of thought and make her desires feel more possible.

As Paola began to feel better and more optimistic, I asked her if she'd taken time to consider what kind of relationship she wanted. We could switch up the crystals she was working with to match the energy of what she desired, increasing her chances of attracting the right guy and having the right relationship. She didn't want to jump into anything too serious, but she did want someone she could get to know, have fun with, and spend some time with on the weekends. I suggested she wear garnet, pink aventurine, and carnelian when she was going out to meet people or on a date, for a sexy, passionate, and fun vibe. I also recommended that she meditate regularly for 5–15 minutes, holding rhodochrosite in her receptive hand and sunstone in her dominant hand to help her manage any insecurities or self-doubts that might come up along the way.

LAW OF ATTRACTION

If you're in a great, happy place, you're likely to attract someone who's in a great, happy place. If you're in an angry, negative, or sad place, you're likely to attract someone who's in an angry, negative, or sad place. Take a good honest look at yourself and do any healing or make any adjustments in mood or perspective to work this law best to your advantage. Hold epidote and a quartz point in your receptive hand and clear topaz and a quartz point in your dominant hand while wearing rubellite over your heart chakra. Sit comfortably in a quiet place, close your eyes, and picture what you want in your mind's eye. Imagine it as if it's already a reality for you and allow yourself to really feel it and enjoy it. Do this for 5–15 minutes daily (or as consistently as possible) until you have achieved your vision. The rubellite connects you to the stronger love vibration, the topaz and epidote dramatically increase your ability to manifest, and the quartz points amplify, magnify, and direct your intentions.

A few weeks later, Paola was happy to report that she had gone from being the "queen of first dates" to the "queen of hot dates," dating not one but two guys who were taking her out regularly, treating her right, and making her feel wonderful. She told me she never goes out without her crystals and is finally enjoying dating for the first time in her life.

Once you can resolve what's holding you back, you can get clear on who you are, your needs and expectations, and the type of relationship you want in your life. It becomes much easier for you to attract that into your experience because you're putting that energy out there and creating a big bull's-eye for Cupid's arrow. It can also save you from a lot of frustrating and dissatisfying experiences along the way. Wear the following crystal combinations daily or as needed (that is, while you're out meeting people or on a date), unless otherwise indicated.

CRYSTAL COMBINATIONS

CASUAL: Wear pink aventurine, carnelian, garnet, and citrine when you're looking for something fun but not serious.

....

DIVINE LOVE: Wear pink kunzite, ajoite, snowflake obsidian, and moonstone when you're looking for a spiritual, like-minded partner, or to attract someone in the spiritual community. You can also meditate regularly holding rubellite in your receptive hand and moonstone in your dominant hand, or sleep with this combination under your pillow.

....

EXCITEMENT: Wear tiger iron, ruby, and emerald when you want an active, adventurous, or athletic relationship.

GETTING CLEAR ON WHAT YOU WANT: Wear sodalite, rhodochrosite, and chrysoprase daily to help you get more in touch with your own inner knowing and to cultivate a greater awareness of your needs, desires, and expectations. You can also meditate while holding sodalite in your receptive hand and azurite in your dominant hand and then journaling about what comes up for you.

INTELLECTUAL STIMULATION: Wear blue sapphire, azurite, and rubellite when you want to attract a partner who is an academic, an intellectual, or a lively conversationalist.

NURTURING AND SUPPORT: Wear mangano calcite, aragonite star cluster, rose quartz, and green aventurine to attract a partner who is a nurturer and will provide you with great emotional support.

ROMANCE: Wear rubellite, rhodonite, and watermelon tourmaline to attract romance or when you're looking for a romantic relationship but want to move slowly.

SEX AND PASSION: Wear garnet, pink aventurine, and ruby to attract someone for a sexy, passionate love affair or a partner with whom you have a great sex life. You can also place these crystals under pillows or by your bed to ignite more passion in a relationship.

TRUST AND FRIENDSHIP: Wear rose quartz, watermelon tourmaline, septarian, and yellow jasper when you want a long-term relationship that's built on friendship, companionship, loyalty, and trust.

SOUL MATES

There's a common misconception that your soul mate is the love of your life, someone who's perfect for you and with whom you'll live for the rest of your life. Actually, soul mates aren't always romantic. They're people who show up in your life to help you learn lessons or who touch you deeply in some way so that you heal, grow, and evolve. They're necessary and important characters in our life stories because they are always meaningful to us (even if we despise them, which may happen!) and they typically prompt great personal change. They may be lovers, but they may also be friends, family, pets, rivals, enemies, or the bane of your existence.

Most people who say they want a soul mate want true love and/or a life partner. The key thing is to be ready for it. With the law of attraction you'll find a partner or relationship that will be a reflection of who you are and where you are in your life at the time. This doesn't mean you have to be perfect! It just means that you need to feel good about yourself and your life, and ready to be in a meaningful, lasting relationship.

Wear rubellite, eudialyte, ajoite, and rhodochrosite regularly to help you attract true love and/or a life partner. If this powerful combination feels too overwhelming, make it into a crystal tonic instead. You can also meditate for 10–30 minutes on a daily basis, holding rose quartz in your receptive hand and eudialyte in your dominant hand, and sleep with rose quartz, rhodochrosite, and rhodonite under your pillow.

If you're like me, you'll probably want all or most of these things! If so, I recommend you do the Law of Attraction exercise on page 58. You may find, though, that when you're really honest with yourself, there are a couple of qualities that matter more to you than the others. If so, you can layer your crystal work by wearing one combination daily and making a crystal tonic of the other.

BREAKUPS

What can I say about breakups that most of us don't already know? They can be very painful or very easy, amicable even, but in my experience each one is a rite of passage. How they're handled, what's expressed (or not), and the willingness to accept change and move on all determine a breakup's emotional impact on the people involved. If you're able to learn from the experience, it can benefit you going forward into your next relationship. And if you work with crystals, they can make it a whole lot easier and help you recover more quickly.

I broke someone's heart once. I wasn't ready for a serious relationship and I knew we weren't well suited to each other, but I also knew he was very much in love with me and so I stayed in the relationship longer than I wanted. I was afraid of hurting him and yet at the same time I really wanted out. When I finally had the courage to bring it up, he was desperate not to let go, wanting to remain friends and clinging to the hope that we had a chance to reunite in the future.

Fortunately, I had opted to wear rose quartz, mangano calcite, and chrysocolla for compassion, gentleness, and authentic expression, and hematite to help me hold my ground. I could have said some very mean things to him to try to push him away and force a clean break, but that would have wounded him and left me feeling terrible. Instead, I was able to communicate to him why it wasn't working and why I felt it best for both of us to go our separate ways. He listened because it was coming from a place of compassion, and while I admit I caved and agreed to the occasional friendly email, he was willing to let go and move on. He was devastated, but at least the whole thing was handled with kindness and sincerity.

CRYSTAL COMBINATIONS

Wear the following crystals on a daily basis, except where otherwise indicated, until you feel they are no longer required.

ACCEPTANCE: Wear mangano calcite, honey calcite, tiger eye, rose quartz, and chrysoprase daily if you're having trouble accepting that a relationship is over and letting go. As an alternative, you can make a crystal tonic of this combination for a more gradual process, or you can meditate, holding mangano calcite in your receptive hand and honey calcite in your dominant hand for 20–30 minutes daily or as needed.

COMPASSION: If you're worried about hurting someone's feelings or saying something you might regret, wear chrysocolla, rose quartz, and mangano calcite. Add optical calcite to the mix for empathy.

COURAGE: Wear aquamarine, amazonite, rhodochrosite, and ruby when you need to summon the courage to instigate or face a breakup.

EXORCISING GHOSTS FROM THE PAST: You've let go, healed, and moved on, but psychically you can feel that your ex hasn't and is still sending vibes your way. Wear black tourmaline, tourmaline quartz, fluorite, labradorite, and rainbow obsidian daily to block this energy intrusion and keep you free from your ex's negative energy.

LETTING GO: They say we all have "the one that got away." Still hanging on to that memory, though, can block you from experiencing new love. Wear or sleep with healer's gold, lepidolite, aquamarine, and hematite regularly until you feel free from the longing.

RECOVERY: If you've been through a rough breakup, wear rhodochrosite, rose quartz, rhodonite, and healer's gold daily. You can also sleep with this combination at night or make a crystal tonic from it.

RELEASING ANGER: If you're still angry with someone who's hurt you, you won't be able to let go, heal, and move forward. No matter how much you say you're over it, if thoughts and memories still upset you, you're not over it. Tony had dated a guy for six months who was domineering, disparaging, prone to angry outbursts, and very negative. When Tony's friends and family started calling his attention to the fact that his boyfriend was mentally and emotionally abusive, Tony thankfully saw the light and ended the relationship.

However, in his mind, Tony still heard the critical and demeaning voice of his ex and would experience a lot of anger and upset when memories flashed through his mind. Anger impedes the healing process: Trapped anger festers inside and becomes bitter over time, binding you to past painful events and never allowing you to truly be free. I suggested that Tony wear amazonite, sunstone, blue kyanite, and sodalite daily to help him get in touch with his anger and to support him in releasing it fully.

After punching many pillows and writing numerous angry letters in all sorts of colorful language (that he subsequently tore up and burned), Tony felt that he had faced his anger sufficiently and was ready to move on. He still wore his crystals, though, because his anger kept resurfacing. He finally realized that he needed to actually send a letter to his ex so that he could speak up for himself and achieve closure. He shared with me later that he felt the crystals had helped keep him honest with himself, and that he was able to express himself in a way that felt eloquent and just when sending his letter. Whether his ex read it or replied didn't matter; what mattered was that Tony was at peace and could truly move on.

....

SADNESS, LOSS, AND GRIEF: Wear or sleep with ruby in fuschite, mangano calcite, and apache tear to support you in healing as well as allowing you to honor your timing and process.

....

SHOCK: Trish was in absolute shock to come home one day and find that her girlfriend of ten years had packed up and left her for another woman. She was still shaking and in complete disbelief when she arrived at our session. I immediately gave her ruby in fuschite to hold in her receptive hand for its restorative effect and angelite in her dominant hand for soothing. After about 15 minutes, the shock began to fade and her emotions started to surface. Tears, denial, anger, and despair all followed, but at least she was able to function again, express her feelings, and face her situation.

···

SILVER LININGS: No matter how badly a relationship went or how much someone hurt you, you can always find some blessing or something you can learn from the experience. It can be hard to seek within for the reason why it happened or what the silver lining might be (especially if the wound is still fresh), but this is what most of us need to do to truly heal, let go, and move forward. When you feel ready to look for the silver lining, meditate on it while holding ajoite in your receptive hand, elestial quartz in your dominant hand, and wearing rhodochrosite, rose quartz, and rhodonite. You may find it helpful afterwards to journal about what came up for you.

HEALING HEARTBREAK

Whether you've lost someone or she broke your heart, the thing that heals us most is time. I've found that working with crystals can help to ease or accelerate this process as well as help you to cope with over-whelming feelings.

Belinda's husband passed away abruptly one night. Even though he was thought to be in prime health—he jogged daily, was a vegetarian, and lived an active lifestyle—he had a massive heart attack while climbing up the stairs to bed and died almost instantly. Belinda was devastated and couldn't understand how it happened or why God had decided to take the man she loved so suddenly. She was still trying to wrap her mind around the fact that she would no longer see him walk into the room, smile, or hold her at night while they slept. She was heartbroken. She went through a period of deep grief and mourning, spending days in bed crying while family and friends would clean the house, walk the dogs, try to get her to eat. Eventually, she roused herself because she knew she had to go on and that her husband would want her to move forward and heal. She asked me which crystals could help her through this time and I recommended mangano calcite for gentle healing and acceptance, amethyst for anxiety and doubt, smoky quartz for grounding and stress relief, and ruby for emotional strength and support.

I do believe that we can fully recover and heal from loss, grief, and heartbreak, but we are forever changed by the experience. In my own times of heartbreak and grief, crystals have been a tremendous source of comfort, support, and healing energy to help me get through my day and honor my process. It's not something you can just snap out of, or repress and move on from, because the feelings and wounds will always be there, and the more they linger, the more they can fester into illness and imbalance. While I say that crystals accelerate the healing process, it's important to understand that I mean they do so by supporting us in allowing us to release our feelings, and by supplying us with the added energy we need to heal. Be gentle with yourself, work with your crystals, and take the time you need.

HEART-HEALING TRINITY

I first read about this crystal combination in Judy Hall's book *The Crystal Bible*. And I have recommended it countless times throughout my career for its epic healing energy. Wear rhodochrosite for healing emotional wounds and resolving old baggage; rose quartz for self-love, nurturing, and support; and rhodonite for the strength, courage, and willingness to open your heart to loving again.

When you're ready to find the blessing in a given situation, wear sodalite, rose quartz, mangano calcite, and aragonite star cluster to help you look within, be honest with yourself, approach things from a loving perspective, accept what happened, and fully embody what you learn so that it can be of benefit to you.

MOVING ON

Sometimes love has gone very wrong for us in the past—we've been in abusive relationships, or we've been betrayed, lied to, robbed, used, or hurt very deeply. Maybe you were in a relationship with an addict or a narcissist, someone who neglected you or even enabled you. Maybe you're recovering from codependency. Maybe you were the abuser. Your first priority is your own healing process, but there will come a point when you'll need to get involved with someone again in order to fully heal and be able to experience a healthier relationship.

I call this next type of relationship a "healing relationship" because it's an opportunity to move forward, to embody what you've learned and how you've grown, and to experience being with someone from a more whole, healthy place. I've supported so many people through this process, and, more than anything, I've observed that it takes a loving commitment to yourself and your process, faith, and sometimes a lot of courage. The feeling of moving forward, of seeing how you've changed and being able to enjoy the kind of relationship you've always wanted, makes it worth it.

Trini was married for ten years to a sex addict. She and her husband first experienced trouble on their honeymoon when he couldn't be aroused without watching porn, and things got worse from there. She eventually gave up trying to make love because he either couldn't become aroused (and would blame her for it), or when he did, she knew he wasn't really present with her. For several long painful years, she blamed herself for her perceived inadequacy while begging him to seek counseling. It all but destroyed her sense of self-worth as a woman.

Finally divorced, she was angry, recovering, and couldn't conceive of being with anyone again. After months of crystal healing, she felt ready to date again, but was understandably timid. How could she trust a man again? Would she really be able to feel sexy and desirable in her own body when being intimate? First, we worked on clarifying Trini's needs—what she was looking for in a man as well as in a relationship. Then as she began to date, we put rose quartz, blue kyanite, hematite, and amethyst in a pouch for her to hold in times when she felt that her trust issues were being triggered or she was afraid or in doubt. This would help her feel calm, acknowledge her feelings, and then make a loving and empowered choice in response.

She started dating a wonderful man who was willing to be patient and supportive as Trini felt her way back into the world of relationships with men. There were bumps in the road to intimacy for Trini, but she was effusive in her praise and gratitude for the crystals that brought her so much comfort and support through that process.

CRYSTAL COMBINATIONS

DESERVING: Feeling you deserve more goes hand in hand with self-worth when your self-worth allows you to receive. Wear green aventurine and rose quartz daily, or meditate holding green aventurine in your receptive hand and rose quartz in your dominant hand regularly for 20–30 minutes.

ENJOYMENT: Allowing yourself to enjoy the process of dating or being in a relationship again makes the whole thing much easier and more fun! Wear pink kunzite, citrine, pink aventurine, and garnet to feel greater pleasure, happiness, and ease.

RESISTANCE: If you feel you're stuck in limbo between having healed from a past relationship but being afraid to be out there in the dating scene again, wear or sleep with watermelon tourmaline, rhodonite, and onyx for the courage, willingness, and loving commitment to get back out there and meet someone.

SELF-ACCEPTANCE: Wear mangano calcite daily or sleep with it at night to accept yourself fully and love yourself more unconditionally.

SELF-LOVE: Wear rose quartz daily or sleep with it at night to cultivate a greater sense of self-love, and a willingness to nurture yourself, honor your needs, and feel better about yourself overall. You can also meditate daily holding rose quartz in both hands for 10–30 minutes.

SELF-WORTH: Wear chrysoprase, honey calcite, and rhodonite on a daily basis when you need to believe more in your own worth and when you want to have greater appreciation and respect for your own value.

....

TRIGGERS: Place ruby in fuschite, lithium quartz, amethyst, hematite, and ruby in a pouch and either wear the pouch or keep it nearby to hold when you feel that old reactionary choices or habits might be triggered by someone or some circumstance.

CHAPTER

Career
and Money

R EMEMBER WHEN YOU WERE ASKED what you wanted to be when you grew up? Maybe your answer was a doctor, or an actor, or an astronaut, or a farmer (I wanted to be magical). It was unlikely that you answered, "I want to be an empowered, healthy, well-adjusted person." What we do for a living doesn't define who we are as individuals, but it certainly shapes our lives and determines part of our contribution to society. We spend a good portion of our lives at work. So if you're not doing something you find fulfilling, profitable, or enjoyable, your life can feel pretty miserable.

I've worked with so many people who were searching for deeper clarity, insight, and guidance in terms of what they were meant to do and their purpose in life. Many of them felt lost, trapped, and disgruntled. Others needed an energy shift to help them find work, or were looking for any edge that could keep them at the top of their game. In each and every case, working with crystals supplied them with the energy they needed to achieve the results they desired.

I remember working with a young woman for over a year who was a salesperson at a high-end clothing store. She had dreams of living somewhere tropical or mountainous but was so overwhelmed with debt and financial obligations that she couldn't see her way out of the concrete jungle. She spent a lot of time and money on socializing and other distractions, which always left her feeling burned out and unfulfilled. In her crystal therapy sessions, we worked a lot with orange calcite and bloodstone to bring her emotional energy back into a state of balance. Ruby for grounding, wealth, and empowerment. Rose quartz for self-love and self-worth. Citrine for optimism. Chrysoprase for self-esteem. Blue sapphire and tiger eye to encourage conscious spending. And azurite for vision.

One day, out of the blue, she was presented with an incredible opportunity: a popular bed-and-breakfast in South America was up for sale, and her mother had some money to invest. Whereas in the past she might have passed on this venture as being impossible or unrealistic, something inside her told her that she could make this work and truly live the life of her dreams. She went for it—and has been loving her life ever since! She credits the crystals with helping her shift her outlook to one of possibility and for giving her the balancing energy she needed to make better choices.

EMPLOYMENT

Looking for a job is a job in itself! Whether you're unemployed or looking for something better, job hunting can take a lot of energy, time, focus, and preparation. It's really important to remain positive, optimistic, focused on what you want, and in a place of positive expectation. Of course, there might be moments when you feel down, rejected, or anxious. Acknowledge these feelings, but then let them pass and shift back to a place of optimism. This will keep you in alignment with your best possible outcome.

Kasia came to see me because she needed an energy shift. She had been out of work for nearly two years. Her severance package and savings had almost run out and she was having no luck in finding a job. She was feeling desperate, afraid, and hopeless. The first thing I did was help relieve her of some of the fear and stress she was feeling by having her wear smoky quartz, black tourmaline, blue kyanite, blue lace agate, and tektite on a daily basis. Whenever she felt negative feelings surfacing, she would grab hold of her crystals and take some deep, slow breaths.

They were legitimate feelings, given her circumstances, but they weren't boosting her chances of finding work.

After a week, she felt better and more in control, so we changed her daily combination to rose quartz for self-worth, chrysoprase and tiger iron for confidence, blue apatite for manifestation, and hematite for conviction and determination. With renewed hope and vigor, Kasia repeated affirmations of success on a daily basis and sent her resumes out with the belief that she was the best candidate for the job. She wore her crystals every day and began interviewing with gusto. She was gainfully employed in just over a month and is now a firm believer that with the right energy, determination, and crystals, anything is possible!

CRYSTAL COMBINATIONS

FINDING A BETTER JOB: If you already have a job but want help finding something better, wear hiddenite for good fortune, eudialyte for alignment with your heart's desires, moldavite for positive transformation, and blue tiger eye for synchronicity and luck in networking.

GOOD LUCK: Sometimes you just need things to go your way a little more. Wear or meditate regularly, holding hiddenite for good luck and good fortune. It will also help to keep your spirits high and your outlook positive as things start shifting for the better.

INTERVIEWING: Go to your interviews wearing fluorite for clarity of thought and insight, blue kyanite for calm and articulate communication, tiger eye for confidence, ruby for self-esteem, and citrine for optimism and positive energy.

JOB-HUNTING: Wear hematite for energy and stamina, amethyst for intuition, tiger iron for motivation, rhodonite to follow your heart's guidance, and blue kyanite for inspiration while seeking and applying for jobs.

NEGOTIATING BENEFITS AND SALARY: This can be very challenging for people who are afraid to ask for more or who struggle with self-worth issues. Spend a full week if you can before the negotiation wearing rose quartz for self-worth, citrine for optimism and prosperity, bloodstone for grounding and abundance, sunstone for confidence and healthy boundaries, and ruby for grounding and empowerment. The time spent with the energy from this crystal combination flowing through you on a daily basis will help shift the negative feelings and limiting self-beliefs that can hold you back. Be sure to wear this combination on the day of your negotiating meeting as well!

SYNCHRONICITY: Being in the right place at the right time or knowing the right person can be the edge you need to get the job. Wear blue tiger eye daily to put yourself in alignment with the flow of synchronous events.

THRIVING

There are many people out there who are grateful just to be employed. Having once been unemployed myself, I can very much appreciate this feeling. Thriving certainly means being able to earn a living and put food on the table, but it also means being able to grow, flourish, and succeed at what you're doing. When I was building my healing business, I worked with crystals daily to help me thrive. Even as I sit here writing these pages, I'm wearing crystals to help keep me in alignment with that energy so that this book can grow and succeed!

The wonderful thing about working with crystals when you're seeking to thrive is that you've got additional energy resources at your disposal. Sometimes we feel as if we have to do it all ourselves or burn the candle at both ends to get things done. Other times we try to stretch ourselves too far to achieve better results. With crystals we're not on our own—we've got renewable sources of awesome energy at our fingertips that can make our lives and work so much more enjoyable and successful.

CRYSTAL COMBINATIONS

ATTRACTING CLIENTS: Wear blue tiger eye, hiddenite, clear quartz, and rhodonite daily to help you attract more clients.

. . . .

CONFRONTATIONS AND CONFLICT RESOLUTION: Hold a piece of hematite in each hand or keep one in a pocket on each side to feel grounded, empowered, and centered when facing a potential conflict or confrontation.

COUNSELORS, THERAPISTS, AND SOCIAL WORKERS:
Wear rose quartz for love and compassion, amethyst for intuition and insight, and jet to keep you from feeling drained by other people's energy.

DEALING WITH A CRUSHING WORK SCHEDULE: I will admit that I'm definitely inclined toward working too hard. This is not an uncommon thing in New York City, especially when you're running your own business! It got to the point where I was working all day, seven days a week, without ever giving myself a break. I'd get up, check my phone, check my emails, work, see clients, do more work, respond to more emails, and then collapse into bed at night. Needless to say, this was not a healthy pace and it was taking a toll on my health and my personal life. Wearing yellow jasper and honey calcite daily, along with taking a crystal tonic made of blue lace agate, helped me bring more balance back to my life. I was better able to honor my limits and establish boundaries so that my personal needs were met, along with my professional needs.

DEALING WITH OVERWHELMING EMOTIONS: Wear ruby in fuschite to help keep your emotional energy balanced and centered, blue lace agate to remain calm and collected, and blue sapphire and fluorite to prioritize and stay on top of things.

FOCUS AND DETERMINATION: Wear onyx, tiger iron, and fluorite as needed, or meditate with fluorite in your receptive hand and tiger iron in your dominant hand for 10 minutes at the start of your day.

CRYSTALS FOR YOUR DESK

I get asked a lot for crystal recommendations for people's offices or cubicles. I have very strategic crystal placements on my desk to ensure optimal working energy. Here are a few of my favorite suggestions:

ACHIEVEMENT: Place a handful of tumbled sunstones in the center of your top desk drawer or in a bowl at the center of your desk.

CALM AND FOCUS: Place a fluorite, amethyst, or smoky quartz sphere near where you sit.

FILTERING ELECTROMAGNETIC SMOG FROM COMPUTERS AND ELECTRONICS: Place a large chunk of either fluorite, black tourmaline, or smoky quartz beside your monitor.

WEALTH: Place pyrite or citrine clusters on the far left-hand corner of your desk.

GETTING A RAISE: Wear green aventurine, sunstone, and bloodstone daily to help gear your energy toward receiving a raise.

......

HEAVY WORKLOAD: Wear red jasper for fortitude, bloodstone for energy, citrine for optimism and inspiration, yellow jasper for realistic pacing, and tiger iron for stamina when you have to plow through a heavy workload or a strenuous workweek ahead.

......

HIGH-STRESS AND HIGH-STAKES ENDEAVORS: Whether it's Fashion Week, tax season, awards season, exam time, pilot season, mergers and acquisitions, or back to school, helping clients through high-stress periods has become a specialty of mine. At times of high stress and heavy workloads, self-care has a tendency to go right out the window. But good self-care enables you to navigate these times most successfully. When downtime is an impossibility, deep restorative sleep (even if only for 3–4 hours) is essential. Place lepidolite under your pillow or fall asleep while holding it in your receptive hand. Wear rose quartz to remind you to eat nourishing foods, sunstone to make it easier when you have to say no, fluorite to keep your head on straight and think quickly on your feet, hematite to give you a strong sense of being anchored, and citrine to keep your energy humming and your face smiling.

......

MINDFUL MANAGEMENT: Wear ruby for leadership, blue sapphire for logical linear thinking, azurite to be able to think outside the box, and aragonite star cluster for fairness when in a management position or for effective group leadership.

MOTIVATION: Meditate with pyrite in your receptive hand and citrine in your dominant hand for 5–10 minutes, as needed.

NETWORKING: Carry blue tiger eye with you when attending networking events to attract and meet influential people.

OPTIMISM: Wear citrine, sunstone, optical calcite, and eudialyte to help you adopt and maintain a positive outlook.

PRESENTATIONS, INTERVIEWS, OR SPEECHES: Wear blue kyanite to articulate thoughts succinctly and aquamarine for courageous, passionate expression. Add fluorite to the mix if you'll need to answer questions on the fly.

PROMOTION: Wear tiger iron, citrine, and jade daily if you're working toward a promotion and to help you receive positive attention and praise.

RESISTANCE AND PROCRASTINATION: Wear blue kyanite and onyx for focus, nuummite for self-mastery, rose quartz for surrender, and hematite for conviction.

SALES: Wear tiger eye, citrine, jade, green aventurine, and bloodstone daily to help you make more sales and boost your overall performance.

TROUBLESHOOTING TECHNICAL DIFFICULTIES: Wear or hold blue kyanite, blue lace agate, and smoky quartz to keep calm and think logically when seeking to troubleshoot or resolve technical difficulties.

....

WRITING, NEGOTIATING, AND SIGNING CONTRACTS: Wear fluorite, blue sapphire, and azurite for strategic thinking, foresight, and to help keep you on top of all the details.

CREATIVITY

A large part of my clientele is people working in the arts, media, and creative industries. Who knows where creative ideas come from? Some say they're born of passion, others necessity. Whether your creative juices spring from the gentle whispers of your heart or if they flow from the Divine, when your rent depends on it, what matters is that they flow! I've seen many a creative block in my time. Lots of crippling self-doubt. And piles of pressure to stay at the top of your game.

I've learned that when you're working in a creative field, nurturing yourself is equally as important as nurturing your muse. The great thing about crystals is that they can help clear creative blocks, boost the flow of creative ideas, and open you up to greater sources of inspiration. All this while supporting your health and well-being, too.

CRYSTAL COMBINATIONS

CREATIVE CRYSTAL SUPPORT TEAM: Wear carnelian, fire agate, jade, citrine, and azurite while working. You can also place larger pieces of these crystals strategically on your desk, in your studio, or in your workshop for added energy.

CREATIVE EXPANSION: If you're ready to expand your ideas, concepts, and creations, meditate with azurite in your receptive hand and cinnabar quartz in your dominant hand regularly for 20–30 minutes. Stay open to whatever guidance or impulses come to you throughout the day.

DIVINE INSPIRATION: Sleep with moonstone under your pillow every night, or meditate holding it in your receptive hand for 10–15 minutes daily. Its yin and intuitive, creative energy are also perfect for plumbing the subconscious for new ideas.

IMAGINATION: The child within us keeps our magic, hope, and wonder alive. Our creative genius, inspired selves, and spark of imagination often come from this special place inside. Meditate or sleep with angelite daily, and wear mangano calcite, pink kunzite, and green aventurine to help tap into the wellsprings of your inner child.

INVITING THE MUSES: Wear pink kunzite, moonstone, and ajoite to relax and bring on a dreamy, expansive state. Give yourself at least one hour wearing this combination while remaining open and receptive, then make note of whatever surfaces. Great guidance and ideas can pop in at times when we just let go and let our minds wander.

PERFORMING: Wear citrine and carnelian for inspired choices, and aquamarine for free, fearless expression when acting, singing, or dancing.

STIMULATION: Wear blue kyanite to stimulate creative expression and ideas.

TRANSDIMENSIONAL IDEAS (ESPECIALLY FOR SPIRITUAL AND SCI-FI/FANTASY ARTISTS AND AUTHORS): Wear celestite for divine inspiration, smoky quartz for grounding and purpose, and cinnabar quartz and ajoite for creative flow and expression.

WORKING UNDER PRESSURE: Wear carnelian, garnet, amethyst, and blue lace agate to keep you from blocking the flow of your creativity or shutting down when you're working under pressure.

WRITER'S BLOCK: Wear carnelian, orange calcite, cinnabar quartz, and citrine daily to dissolve creative blocks and get your good chi flowing again.

SUCCESS

They say true success is being happy. Are you happy with what you're doing for a living? If you're consistently experiencing anxiety Sunday night, and the Monday morning blues, my guess is you're not. Do you dream of doing something else? Is there potential you've yet to tap into or greatness you've yet to explore? Maybe you love what you do and you want to do it better. The right crystals can help you tap into your own inner knowing, guidance, and soul's vision so that you can succeed in pursuing and achieving your dreams.

CRYSTAL COMBINATIONS

ACHIEVING GOALS: Wear moldavite, eudialyte, tiger iron, citrine, and nuummite when working toward achieving your goals. Note that the more specific, realistic, and time-based your goals are, the more achievable they become.

SKIRTING ROADBLOCKS: No matter how much you might be in alignment with your guidance, inspired by your visions, on track with your goals, or even have forged the best-laid plans, you're still likely to experience challenges, roadblocks, detours, or delays. This can understandably bring you down or frustrate you. Wear citrine for optimism and energy, garnet for passion and inner strength, blue kyanite for insight and wisdom, and eudialyte for loving motivation to boost your morale and keep you moving forward (even if you have to zigzag your way to your goal).

VISION

As long as you're in survival mode, you'll stay there. Only when you have a vision of where you want to go, what you want to achieve, and who you want to be is something greater guiding your choices. Vision is not something you can force yourself to figure out. It has to be something that comes from deep inside your soul—something that excites and inspires you, something that revs up your passion to succeed.

Wear a Herkimer diamond daily to help guide you to this inner wisdom, and meditate regularly, holding celestite in your receptive hand and eudialyte in your dominant hand. Holding these two crystals will help you access your own inner wisdom and be open to receiving soul-level guidance. Have something on hand so you can take notes. Ask yourself what you really want to do for a living or ask for guidance or action steps that can help you pursue your goal. Let the images, thoughts, and messages float up to you. Don't judge or censor or dismiss what you're receiving. Make notes and ask yourself more questions until you feel complete or feel the need to stop.

This may require more than one session. But the more you do this work, the more your own inner wisdom will come through to you clearly.

WORKING SMARTER, NOT HARDER: Wear or meditate daily with blue sapphire, sodalite, and fluorite when seeking to simplify, delegate, or automate tasks so that your energy and attention can be applied more effectively.

MONEY

Along with crystal healing, I also do Akashic Record readings for people (channeling soul-based guidance from the Universe), and I have observed that the two most common topics for which people seek guidance are love and money. Whether you're on a salary, have a fixed income, do freelance work, or work as an entrepreneur, there are always ways and means to attract more money. We've all heard of the rich uncle passing away, but there are so many other random or intentional ways you can earn or receive cash, build wealth, and prosper. Investment opportunities, side jobs, promotions, prize winnings, and boosts in sales are all perfect examples. You can work really hard for it, or work smart with crystals to give you an edge.

Along with having a positive influence on your own energy, crystals work the Law of Attraction ("like attracts like") and the Law of Similars ("like cures like") to your benefit. A good thing to remember about the Law of Attraction is that it's perfect and absolute. It's always in operation and it doesn't differentiate between right and wrong, good and bad, light and dark, and the like. The same is true with crystals. A thief can apply this work as effectively as a saint: It's not about what or how much you want or even how you go about getting it. It's all about how you direct your energy of intent and the quality of your vibration. Of course, it bears mentioning that the Law of Karma is also perfect. My point is that there's no one judging whether or not you're worthy or whether or not it's possible except for yourself.

A lot of people get in their own way when doing this work. This is simply a matter of influencing the quality of your energy and its direction to flow in accordance with your desires, intentions, or purpose. Counsel yourself to remain in a place of expectation and willingness to receive. If you secretly think you're not worthy or that it won't work, you'll be blocking the energy from flowing to achieve your purpose.

If you're in a really tight spot financially, and have no hope of shifting circumstances in your favor, faith can be your trump card. Choosing to have faith in the possibility that things can improve is enormously powerful because it allows for that opportunity. If you give it a chance, universal or divine energy can provide for you seemingly from out of thin air. I've had many instances when I didn't know how I was going to make it through the month. Then a client would arrange for a series of healing sessions, or I'd discover I had more money in my bank account than I had thought, or I'd book a slew of new client appointments. I was willing to have faith that somehow I'd be provided for and, as a result, I always was. Don't question how it will happen because that can introduce doubt. Just thank God when it does and celebrate!

Numerous crystals will help you attract more money. Many of them vibrate on the same frequencies as wealth, money, fortune, currency, and abundance, so they will attract like frequencies. They'll also influence your energy vibration to encourage more success and to balance or dissolve energy that can block abundance. You can work with each crystal individually or combine one with several others according to your needs.

CRYSTAL COMBINATIONS

ABUNDANCE: Wear green aventurine daily if you're constantly giving but not receiving enough. This can block you from manifesting abundance because your energy is always going out without enough flowing back in. Think of a well: If you're constantly emptying a well without replenishing the source, it will eventually run dry. This creates an energy imbalance that will inevitably show up in every area of your life, including your finances. If you feel as if you're working solely to make ends meet or that you have too many expenses, then your energy is likely imbalanced. You can also meditate holding green aventurine in your receptive hand and tiger eye in your dominant hand for 15 minutes daily until your energy is more balanced. This will encourage an increased flow of abundance in your direction.

GOOD FORTUNE: Meditate while holding chrysanthemum stone in your receptive hand for 20 minutes daily when you're seeking to shift or improve your fortunes. You can also place it on a money altar, in your wealth corner if you practice feng shui, or hold it periodically in your receptive hand to enhance your wealth vibration. It's a clay-based stone so you have to be careful with it if you choose to wear it, as it can crack or break easily if dropped. This is a great stone to work with regularly for building and maintaining wealth.

LUXURY: Wear or meditate with ruby daily when you want to be at the top of your game and living a lifestyle of comfort, wealth, and luxury. Ruby is a stone of wealth, money, royalty, pleasure, and success. Its energy is empowering, grounding, and expansive. Ruby is the crystal to work with when you know what you want and you know how you want it. Its energy can help you build wealth in the form of assets, objects, and beautiful things.

....

MONEY CLEARING: I often teach my clients and students to clear their money because it absorbs all kinds of energy. Currency floats around from person to person and place to place. It can carry the vibrations of fear, resentment, greed, longing, despair, and indulgence. That $20 in your hand could have been the last money a mother had to buy her children food, it could have been exchanged in a drug deal, or it could have been used to pay off a gambling debt. Don't carry those vibes with you! Place selenite nightly on your money to neutralize its energy and then charge your money with positive intentions. You can do this very quickly by holding it in your dominant hand and imagining feelings of plenty and gratitude flowing into your money. This is a simple yet powerful way to boost your abundance vibration.

....

MONEY FEAR: Hold or wear tektite, as needed, when you are suffering from intense money fear. There have been times in my life when I've had my phone service disconnected and been too broke to afford food. As I started building my crystal healing business and getting back on my feet, I would be hit with intense money fear. How would I survive? Would I be able to pay my bills at the end of the month? Will I ever make it or will I end up on the street? It doesn't matter if the fear you're feeling is justified. Fear keeps you trapped in poverty and a lack mentality, which makes it much harder for you to improve your circumstances. When your energy is being invested in fear, you'll attract fearful circumstances. Tektite helps to weaken fear's hold on you so that your efforts to achieve prosperity stand a greater chance of success.

....

MONEY MAGNET: Meditating regularly while holding cinnabar quartz in your receptive hand for 20–30 minutes will help draw wealth into your life very quickly. Cinnabar is formed from mercury sulfide, so it's toxic and needs to be handled very carefully. It sometimes forms naturally in quartz, though there's a lot of lab-formed specimens on the market. Either formation proves to be a powerful combination because the quartz forms a protective casing for the cinnabar and magnifies and intensifies its properties. I bought a powerful piece of this crystal combination in Sedona, Arizona, and have found it most effective to meditate while holding it near my solar plexus chakra (the fire in your belly). This crystal works rapidly and has a very expansive energy, so you may find that wearing it on a daily basis can be overwhelming.

....

POVERTY MENTALITY: When all you perceive, affirm, or expect is lack, then you are demonstrating poverty mentality. Wear emerald daily if you struggle with poverty mentality, feeling unworthy of wealth, or feeling that you are incapable of improving your circumstances. Emerald nurtures and expands our highest feelings and loving opinions of ourselves. It also attracts wealth and abundance. You can also meditate while holding it in your receptive hand or sleep with it several times a week. You don't need to work with gem-grade emerald to benefit from its effects. Other grades will work just as well, though you'll need larger pieces (minimum 1½"/3.8cm) to have the same potency as a gem-grade emerald.

PROSPERITY: Wearing jade to attract prosperity and good fortune is especially beneficial for those who are pursuing their dreams, life purpose, or self-mastery. Jade increases your appreciation for the finer things in life and helps you develop an awareness of the abundance that is available to us all. It curtails feelings of jealousy and competitiveness that can underlie a lack, or poverty, mentality. Jade is worked with best on a daily basis in the form of adornment (for example, jewelry), but can also be effective held in the receptive hand while meditating or placed on altars for luck and divine intervention.

REDUCING DEBT: Debt is a form of slavery because it can tie up so much of our energy and resources. Debt is a huge source of stress and worry for many people and can feel overwhelmingly restrictive. Wear blue sapphire if you're working on managing or reducing your debt. It helps you make choices that are in alignment with your goals while also helping to minimize any fears or worries you have surrounding your debt. Wearing blue sapphire can help you keep things in perspective and feel in control so that you can put more of your energy and resources toward higher feelings and intentions.

RESOURCES: Wear or sleep with bloodstone if you have a lot of great money-generating ideas or projects, but struggle to bring them to fruition. Bloodstone attracts wealth in the form of resources that can support the attraction and accumulation of more wealth and bolster the success of your business ideas and projects. Ideas are just ideas until they're grounded energetically in the material (physical) plane, where they can then take root and grow. Bloodstone helps to anchor your passions in reality so that they can be pursued successfully (rather than just fizzling out). Bloodstone has a slow and steady vibration so it's best to wear it for long periods, rather than just holding it in meditation.

SPENDING WISELY: Tiger eye is a must-wear when shopping, making investments, building a business, or spending money. I know a few shopaholics, and their money flies right out the door as soon as they've earned it. Spending can be glorious fun, but when money's going out all the time, it can create an energy imbalance that will constantly keep you in the red. Tiger eye has a grounding, centering, balancing influence that can help you to stop and think twice before charging something on that credit card. Meditating with tiger eye can also help you form better boundaries with yourself and empower you in honoring them.

SUCCESS: Placing pyrite at your desk, near the cash register in your shop, or in your workspace stimulates an improved work ethic, heightens ambition, and attracts wealth and abundance. A large chunk of it can also be placed in your wealth corner, if you practice feng shui, or on a wealth altar. Meditating while holding pyrite in your receptive hand and visualizing the amount of money, business, or prosperity you want to attract helps to bring it into your experience more quickly. If you want to wear pyrite throughout the day, do so with awareness, as it can increase feelings of competitiveness or aggressive behavior, which may or may not work to your advantage.

UNIVERSAL WEALTH: Work with citrine if you want wealth to come to you in the highest frequency of integrity and by divine right (meaning that your wealth isn't gained through harm or to the detriment of another). Citrine works especially well if you're seeking to profit from creative, artistic, or spiritual ventures. You can wear citrine daily to attract abundance and good fortune or place it in your wallet, cash register, tip jar, place of business, or shop window to attract more money, business, and sales. If you practice feng shui, it can be placed in the wealth corner of your home or business to help attract abundance, prosperity, and positive energy. Meditating with citrine not only enhances your own wealth vibration, but it can also stimulate ideas or draw in divine inspiration in terms of generating more wealth. Wearing citrine regularly will also help you cultivate a greater sense of prosperity consciousness and possibility. It can be paired with amethyst in your place of business if you feel that negative energy is hampering your success.

CHAPTER
6

Physical Health and Travel

THROUGHOUT MY YEARS of offering crystal healing, I have had the fortunate experience of helping people cope with myriad health issues, illnesses, and ailments. I have to admit that, at first, even I was skeptical that crystal energy could help the body heal. In my own personal process, I had turned to crystals for emotional and spiritual support, not physical healing, yet upward of 50 percent of my clientele were people either seeking out alternative forms of health care or were coming to see me because nothing else was working in treating their physical ailments. These clients were consistently reporting significantly positive results, so much so that I felt encouraged to document my sessions over time and to use crystals for my own health and healing.

A chiropractor came to one of my crystal healing workshops, proclaiming himself to be a skeptic but noting that he was attending at the behest of his friend. He had suffered from chronic lower back pain for twenty-three years and challenged me to offer him some relief using crystals. I placed large pieces of selenite on his lower back, along with two pieces each of red jasper and hematite for roughly 40 minutes. After the healing he remarked that his back did feel better, but that he wanted to wait and see if the relief lasted. Two days later he called me. He was utterly amazed and eager to learn more about crystal healing because he was no longer experiencing any pain in his back!

The main thing to remember when using crystals for physical health and healing is that they need to be placed as locally as possible (meaning either on or close to the area that is injured, unwell, or imbalanced), and as consistently as possible until the issue has been resolved. Sometimes, the effects of crystals may be immediate; other times, it may take days or weeks of repeated applications to promote the healing or recovery process. It all depends on the extent and seriousness of your injury or illness. Always honor what you're feeling and trust your body's response to crystal therapy.

All the following crystal suggestions come from my session notes and had positive results for my clients. It's by no means an exhaustive list, but these were the most common issues crystals helped to address and what I felt would be the most relevant to readers. Please note that I have chosen to omit work done for serious illness (such as cancer, HIV, and heart disease) because much of that work was focused on underlying emotional causes as opposed to physical causes.

INJURIES

With injuries you can use crystals to manage pain, reduce swelling and inflammation, and accelerate your body's natural healing process. To do this work effectively, you need to choose one crystal from each one of the categories described starting on the next page. Even if a crystal shows up in more than one category, make sure that you're always working with at least three and at most nine crystals depending on the severity and size of your injury. If you can't place them locally, hold one for either pain or inflammation (whichever one feels more relevant) in your receptive hand and one for accelerated healing in your dominant hand. Work with your crystals, as needed, until the injury has healed.

Sometimes you have to get a little creative in terms of your crystal placements, depending on the area of injury. I have repetitive strain injuries in both my shoulders from years of grueling swim practice when I was a teenager. I now carry the bulk of my stress and tension in my shoulders and can reinjure them pretty easily. Whenever I'm in pain,

I slide flat pieces of selenite under my bra straps to help ease tension and reduce the pain. It's quick, convenient, and I start to feel relief in seconds! My mother suffers from arthritic pain in her knees and will wrap bandages around them and then slide selenite sticks in there while watching TV or reading. She swears the only time she's pain-free is when she's got her selenites on her knees.

PAIN

I consider selenite second only to an ice pack for addressing pain. It's fast and effective and 100 percent natural. Sometimes its effects will last long after the selenite has been removed from the area of injury because it has dissolved blocked chi in the area (blocked chi is a common cause of pain). I have pieces of selenite in various shapes and sizes in my healing kit, specifically for localized pain relief.

Other crystals to be used for pain relief include black tourmaline, lepidolite, lithium quartz, blue calcite, hematite, celestite, and rose quartz.

SWELLING AND INFLAMMATION

My first choice for swelling and inflammation is always celestite. It can visibly reduce swelling and inflammation in as little as 30 minutes. In my experience, while swelling will resolve more quickly, inflammation, especially if it's chronic, can take longer and require more crystal applications.

It's important to remember that you are only addressing the symptoms of swelling and inflammation with crystal energy. You still have to resolve the cause. If your foot's swollen because it has a piece of glass in it, or if you have gut inflammation from food intolerances, simply using a crystal will not suffice. The point is to support your healing process, not mask uncomfortable symptoms.

If the locality or source of the inflammation is unclear, you can hold your crystal in your receptive hand until you notice a decrease in symptoms.

Other crystals used for swelling and inflammation include selenite, bloodstone, black tourmaline, aquamarine, angelite, blue calcite, and chrysocolla.

ACCELERATING HEALING

Malachite is a powerful accelerator of the body's natural healing process. I have used it for everything from a torn medial meniscus in my right knee to respiratory infections, sprains, and even PMS! Malachite is quite toxic if ingested, so please don't place it in your bath or drinking water. It is safe for topical use, especially when polished or tumbled. As a general commonsense caution, never place crystals on open wounds.

Celestite is another wonderful healing accelerator. Years ago I sprained my hand (a real problem when you earn a living from hands-on healing!) and I needed to recover quickly so that I could get back to work. I can't remember why I was guided to hold a large chunk of it in my injured hand while sleeping, but after three nights in a row, my hand was completely back to normal. After that experience, I was convinced of celestite's healing power and use it regularly to great effect with my clients.

Other crystals for accelerated healing include hematite, red jasper, healer's gold, green aventurine, green calcite, bloodstone, and tiger iron.

ILLNESSES AND AILMENTS

Again this is by no means an exhaustive list, but these were common issues experienced by many of my clients over the years. If you feel intuitively drawn to working with crystals other than the ones mentioned here, go for it. Be mindful of your body's divine intelligence when it comes to healing: If something doesn't feel right to you or it isn't proving to be effective, then discontinue its use. It's also possible to experience adverse effects from crystal energy, but all the suggestions below were used repeatedly throughout years of my healing sessions and consistently yielded successful results.

CRYSTAL COMBINATIONS

ADRENAL FATIGUE: Wear chrysocolla, ocean jasper, citrine, and green aventurine on a daily basis. You can also make this combination into a crystal tonic (see Chapter 11, "Crystal Tonics," on page 207).

AFTERNOON PICK-ME-UP: Hold a shiva lingam in your receptive hand or pop one in your pocket or in your bra. I like to think of shiva lingams as little battery boosts of crystal energy.

APPETITE CONTROL: Wear blue apatite when eating to help control and/or reduce your appetite. As an overeater in recovery, I can especially swear by this crystal's ability to quell my appetite, particularly during times when I feel triggered or late at night when I had a tendency to overindulge.

ARTHRITIS: Place angelite, malachite, and hematite on the afflicted area for a minimum of one hour daily.

....

BACK PAIN: Place pieces of black tourmaline, selenite, red jasper, and hematite on your back while lying down for one hour regularly, or as needed. If it's too painful for you to lie down on your front, you can tape flat pieces of selenite and wear them over the affected area throughout the day. It might sound silly, but I've found this works better than taking meds, and it's 100 percent natural.

....

BLOOD PRESSURE (HIGH): Wear lithium quartz, blue lace agate, and hematite daily. If you find that this combination mellows you out too much, use pink opal instead of lithium quartz.

....

BURNOUT (RECOVERY FROM): Combine green aventurine, red calcite, ruby, amethyst, and smoky quartz in a small fabric pouch and wear or hold it to gently start restoring your system while at rest. You can also make a crystal tonic from this combination.

....

CONSTIPATION: Wear apache tear, snowflake obsidian, red jasper, and rhodonite as needed. You can also make a crystal tonic of this combination. As a side note, I often found that clients who had regularity issues also had control issues. If this resonates for you, your regularity issue could in fact be a result of emotional issues that need to be addressed and healed.

DETOX (IN SUPPORT OF A DETOX HEALTH PROGRAM):
Wear red and orange calcite, rhodonite, jet, and tourmaline quartz daily for the duration of the program to help your body detox.

ENERGY/VITALITY: Wear tiger iron, ruby, citrine, gold or copper rutilated quartz, and shiva lingam for more energy.

EXERCISE: Wear tiger iron, red jasper, and citrine for increased motivation to work out and to have more energy, stamina, and strength while exercising. Wearing this combination regularly may also accelerate weight loss.

FERTILITY (PROMOTING): Place carnelian, shiva lingam, ruby, and copper rutilated quartz over the womb 2–3 times a week.

FIBROIDS (UTERINE): I have several clients who see me on a monthly basis to help relieve fibroid symptoms during their menstrual cycle. After placing large pieces of celestite over their wombs for 30–45 minutes, there's visible reduction in the bloating/inflammation caused by my clients' fibroids and they consistently report feeling free of any pain or discomfort.

FOOD POISONING (RECOVERY FROM): Wear red calcite to help detoxify the body and hematite for nausea.

HANGOVER: Wear fluorite to clear mental fog and orange calcite to help detoxify and revitalize the body, and hold selenite wherever it hurts.

HEADACHE/MIGRAINE: Place a large piece of either celestite, selenite, or blue calcite as close to the epicenter of pain as possible, until the pain subsides. As an alternative you can hold it in your receptive hand.

HEARING IMPAIRMENT: Hold a piece of quartz in your dominant hand and concentrate on your intention of being able to hear more clearly and accurately. Wear the quartz whenever your hearing needs a boost. Clear once a week and then recharge it with your intention.

HORMONAL BALANCE: Wear moonstone and chrysocolla daily.

IMMUNE SYSTEM SUPPORT (OPTION #1): Wear red jasper, honey calcite, citrine, green aventurine, and green calcite daily. You can also make a crystal tonic of this combination.

IMMUNE SYSTEM SUPPORT (OPTION #2): Wear orange calcite and citrine throughout the day for added immune support.

INDIGESTION: Place fire agate, citrine, orange calcite, sunstone, and tiger iron over the stomach and intestinal area for 30–60 minutes.

INTESTINAL INFLAMMATORY ISSUES: Place celestite, aquamarine, malachite, bloodstone, and hematite over the affected area for one hour regularly or as needed.

NAUSEA: Hold hematite to ease feelings of nausea, dizziness, or vertigo. You can also rub or hold the hematite to the inside of the wrist for fast-acting nausea relief. I keep a piece of hematite on hand when I'm flying for this very reason; it's saved me from having to use an in-flight barf bag more than once!

OVARIAN CYSTS: Miriam was facing the possibility of surgery for her ovarian cysts. She had previously experienced a few ruptures and her doctor was concerned that she would have more complications. Miriam was determined to try some natural or alternative routes before opting for surgical solutions. We worked regularly in her crystal therapy sessions with celestite, malachite, sugilite, chrysocolla, and smoky quartz, placing these crystals over the approximate location of her cysts for 45 minutes at a time. Miriam had been told that her cysts could not diminish in size and would only grow larger, so both she and her doctor were shocked to discover that after three months her cysts had shrunk. Miriam was convinced that the crystals were responsible for this wonderful result and was grateful that she had given them a try.

PREGNANCY (SUPPORT DURING): It is very important that an expectant mother go light on crystals throughout all three trimesters to avoid adversely affecting her unborn child. Never place crystals on the womb, except for jet, and only if there is concern that the baby has absorbed some of the mother's stress. You can wear red calcite or ruby for vitality, stamina, and strength; jet or smoky or rose quartz for stress relief; rhodochrosite if you're having fears around childbirth or are in the process of healing your own childhood wounds; amethyst for anxiety, stress, or worry. For sciatica, back pain, and muscle tension, massaging locally with a selenite massage wand can bring rapid relief. Wearing or meditating while holding rose quartz will strengthen the loving bond between mother and child. And, as a general rule, calcites of any color are usually gentle enough to be worn daily to help address any additional symptoms.

PREMENSTRUAL SYNDROME (PMS): Place selenite, malachite, red jasper, celestite, and hematite over the womb area or on the lower back for a maximum of one hour or until symptoms subside. I had a client who would schedule an appointment with me every month before the start of her period because she experienced at most only mild PMS symptoms after a session with this crystal combination.

RESPIRATORY ILLNESSES: Place blue calcite, selenite, emerald, green calcite, and malachite on the chest daily until the illness subsides.

SHOULDER/NECK TENSION: Tape flat pieces of selenite to the backs of your shoulders or slide them under your bra straps for quick relief of pain and tension.

SLEEP (ANXIOUSNESS): Hold angelite in your receptive hand while falling asleep or place it under your pillow if you find that anxiousness or overthinking is keeping you awake.

SLEEP (DISRUPTED PATTERNS): Meditate with mookaite jasper for 5–10 minutes before bed and then place it at the bottom of your receptive foot for the night. It will help to adjust your body's natural sleep cycle if you have to work odd hours or if you're trying to adjust to a new sleep routine.

SLEEP (FALLING BACK ASLEEP): If you find that you have a tendency to wake up in the middle of the night and then have trouble falling back to sleep, hold rose quartz in your receptive hand for 5 minutes while focusing only on your breathing. Rose quartz is soothing to the system and can help you slip back into your circadian rhythm relatively quickly. I often experience this problem and keep a polished piece of rose quartz beside my bed specifically for this purpose.

SLEEP (INSOMNIA): Hold lepidolite in your receptive hand until you feel sleepy, then place it either under your pillow or by the top of your head for the night.

SORE THROAT: Place blue calcite on the throat or wear it around your neck until the pain subsides.

SPORTS: Wear hematite, sunstone, ruby, and citrine for increased energy, stamina, and focus during competitions.

STRESS (OPTION #1): Wear, bathe, or meditate with smoky quartz to clear excess stress from your system. You can also sleep with smoky quartz placed by the bottom of your dominant foot (the foot on the dominant side of your body) at night.

STRESS (OPTION #2): Hold selenite in your receptive hand and black tourmaline in your dominant hand to clear or neutralize stress in your system. This can be done for 20 minutes while in meditation, watching TV, at the hairdresser, on the subway, and the like.

VIRILITY: Wear fire agate, pyrite, red jasper, and tiger iron in your pant pockets, or make a crystal tonic of the combination and take a dose 3–5 times daily, to boost virility and healthy sexual function.

....

WEIGHT LOSS: Wear blue apatite, citrine, green aventurine, blue kyanite, and bloodstone on a daily basis, as needed. Can also be worn periodically after successful weight loss to help you maintain a healthy weight.

TRAVEL

It goes without saying that I never leave home without crystals. Whether I'm just going to the grocery store, out of state, or overseas, I'm always wearing crystals. When traveling with crystals, one of the main considerations is to keep it light—there's nothing like dragging around a bag full of rocks (believe me, I know!). Functionality, practicality, and priority are the things you want to focus on when making your travel selections, just as you would with clothing and other paraphernalia.

I always keep my crystals in my carry-on luggage. I make sure that they're packed securely but that they're also easily accessible if I want to grab one. I find that packing them in cloth pouches, either individually or in small, themed groups (e.g., your jet lag crystals and calming crystals), works best. Stick with smaller tumbled or rough crystals, as opposed to sticks, wands, or pointed specimens, as they can be seized by transportation security agents as potential bludgeoning or stabbing instruments. Seriously. If you want to pack any of that variety, you'll need to do so in your checked luggage. I've found wrapping them in some paper towels and then placing them in small poster tubes keeps them safe from cracking or breaking.

If you're highly sensitive to energy and/or empathic, be aware that hotel rooms can be full of imbalanced chi and psychic debris that can lead to a disturbed night's sleep. In many places, burning sacred smoke isn't an option, due to hotel regulations, but what you can do is use a crystal tuning fork or singing bowl to help improve the chi and clear the energy of the space. I travel with a tuning fork everywhere I go for that reason. I also always place a few crystals under my pillow and beside the bed for extra protection and support.

CRYSTAL COMBINATIONS

AFFABILITY: Wear ocean jasper, citrine, and sunstone to have an open, relaxed, and easy disposition.

ANXIETY AND STRESS (REDUCING): Wear amethyst and smoky quartz to help soothe your nerves and keep your system mellow. Amethyst will also keep your thoughts from heading into negative or fearful places.

EXTRA ENERGY: Wear red jasper, hematite, and citrine to help you stay awake or for an extra energy boost.

INTUITION AND FOCUS: Wear labradorite, kyanite, and amethyst to remain alert and in tune with your surroundings, and to make the best split-second decisions.

JET LAG (ALLEVIATING): Wear or meditate in the morning with mookaite jasper and shiva lingam until your system adjusts and you feel recovered from jet lag.

....

JOY AND LUCK: Yes, you can be that person who gets the free room upgrade, is seated next to the cute single passenger, arrives in plenty of time for her connection, scores an invite to the party on the yacht, and so on. Carry or wear jade, hiddenite, and pink opal. This combination helps you to feel good and happy, and keeps you in sync with the flow of the Universe. You can add in blue tiger eye to help you meet influential people and to find yourself always in the right place at the right time.

....

PROTECTION: Wear or hold black tourmaline, labradorite, blue kyanite, and black obsidian to shield you from negative vibes and help to intuitively guide you away from potentially harmful people or situations.

....

ROMANCE: Wear rubellite, pink aventurine, and carnelian daily if you're hoping to experience some romance on your vacation.

....

UNDISTURBED SLEEP: For sleep disruptions due to psychic debris, imbalanced energy, or spirits in your room, place a piece of selenite, black tourmaline, celestite, blue kyanite, and lepidolite under your pillow or beside your bed. Sadly, this combination will not help you drown out the noise from the frat party in the adjoining room, but it should help shield you from any etheric problems. Please note that as celestite is fragile, you will need to pack it in its own separate, padded pouch or container to keep it from being damaged while traveling.

CHAPTER

Mental and Emotional Healing

SPECIALIZE IN MENTAL and emotional healing with crystals because in my own personal process that's what I've needed from them most. I always tell my students that, as healers, our lives are our school: We learn best to heal what we need to heal for ourselves. I've struggled with anxiety, depression, and anger issues since I was a child, and I admit that, even to this day, I don't handle stress very well. I had my first anxiety attack at eighteen, and my first breakdown when I was twenty-four. When I moved to New York City, I stopped taking the antidepressants I was on, but then steadily developed a habit of self-medicating with food and booze. When my life hit the skids at the age of thirty, I finally started reaching out for real help. This is what drew me to the world of spiritual healing, where I had my first official introduction to the healing power of crystals.

We've made great strides throughout the centuries in treating physical maladies, but when it comes to mental and emotional health and well-being, our knowledge is still growing. The majority of my clients who are seeking mental and emotional healing had tried therapy and pills, but found that they were still struggling and were getting tired of just talking about it. They wanted change, and they didn't want it to take another ten years. I know that feeling because I've been there; my recovery was a long road, but without my crystals I don't think I would have made it. I turned to them first and foremost to help soothe my anxiety and manage my stress, but also for the fortitude and resilience I needed to pull through a very hard time in my life. I then worked with them to help heal my emotional wounds, to boost my sense of self-worth, to increase my intuition so that I could start making better choices and find my way, to stop self-medicating, to have courage when I felt afraid, to give me optimism when I felt defeated and confidence when I felt hopelessly insecure and worthless.

Am I perfect now? Heck, no! I'm my own favorite fixer-upper, and I'll have things to work on, heal, and change until the day I die (and beyond), and that's true for all of us. When you finally reach that point of enlightened perfection, where you have nothing left to learn or heal, that's when you get to join the Buddha and the big J.C. up there in the sky. Until then, don't worry—you're in good company with the rest of humanity. But if you're working with crystals, you've got a lot of help and support at your disposal. Crystals won't magically wipe away your pain, change you overnight, or erase your mistakes, but they can provide you with the energy you need to help you become a better, healthier, happier, and more healed and whole human being.

BAD HABITS, NEGATIVE PATTERNS, AND HARMFUL BEHAVIORS

To shift or change a pattern of choice or behavior in your life, like always falling for guys who cheat on you, working a job for three months and then quitting, or having that one drink too many, it's important to first recognize the pattern, accept it without judgment, and then identify the root cause. Once you understand why you're doing something, you can then figure out how to resolve it. Sometimes simply replacing the behavior does the trick, like meditating with a crystal when you're anxious, rather than biting off all your nails or inhaling a bag of chips. The root cause of your nail-biting habit is anxiety and, if you know this, you are empowered to make a different choice in response to it and therefore resolve the problem. There are times, though, when that root cause needs to be addressed, as in patterns of abuse when the abused becomes the abuser, or in cases of addiction, self-sabotage, or patterns of unhealthy relationships. In cases like those, replacing the behavior is only masking the problem, rather than resolving it.

Elizabeth was the owner of a trendy gastropub, and had a history of dating guys who were heavy or habitual drinkers. She had moved on to a new and promising relationship after leaving her ex-boyfriend, an alcoholic who had to get up in the middle of the night to take a shot of vodka to keep him from going into withdrawal. Elizabeth was working with me to manage her stress because she was concerned that her current beau also had a problem: He wasn't as bad as her ex, but he would occasionally binge drink and then come home plastered and unruly, and if Elizabeth said anything to him about it, it resulted in a big fight, with him being verbally abusive toward her. The next day he would apologize profusely and promise that it would never happen again, but then a couple of weeks later he'd be back out at the local bar, and they'd go through it all again.

Elizabeth felt that dating drinkers was simply a professional hazard—it hadn't occurred to her that it was actually a pattern that needed to be resolved. We worked with sodalite for introspection, mangano calcite for acceptance, and black obsidian to help bring the root cause to the surface of her awareness. She finally made the connection: When she was a child, her father had died of cirrhosis, but prior to that she had always tried to care for him and appease him when he was drunk and raging throughout the house. It had been very traumatizing for her and she had blocked the memories from her mind. The trauma needed to be healed, so her subconscious kept drawing her to the same situation over and over again to help bring it to her attention.

CRYSTAL COMBINATIONS

ACCEPTANCE: Accepting that you have a problem may be challenging, because it means owning a truth that for reasons of fear or shame you would prefer to deny. Gentle acceptance, without the pressure of that fear, shame, or self-judgment, supports you in moving forward in your healing process. Wear or meditate daily with moonstone and mangano calcite to cultivate gentle acceptance.

ADDICTION AND BREAKING BAD HABITS: Wear rhodochrosite, amethyst, and hematite daily for emotional support. You can also make a crystal tonic from this combination, and sleeping with rose quartz can be beneficial.

COMMITMENT: I have to admit that due to some of my own unfortunate childhood experiences, I have a real problem with the word "discipline." I prefer the word "commitment" in its place, because it feels more empowering, rather than imposing. Wear or meditate daily with onyx, hematite, and rubellite to help you make and keep loving commitments to yourself.

PATTERN RECOGNITION: When you suspect, or it's suggested to you, that you are caught up in an unhealthy pattern or cycle of behavior, wear or hold sodalite while journaling or meditating on it to help you recognize the pattern and deduce its underlying cause.

SHADOW SELF HEALING

Your shadow self contains all the parts of yourself that you don't like and/or won't acknowledge, and beliefs formed in your childhood that may still be governing your thoughts and behaviors in a counterproductive way. It's the part of yourself that uses your fears and sense of shame against you.

Unless you're willing to look at the shadow part of yourself, you may never be aware that it's at work when you choose: to settle for second best; keep eating when you should stop; or give up before you start because you don't think it will work out anyway. The cause of bad habits or harmful behaviors can most likely be found in your shadow self.

For years I struggled to lose weight. It was only when I finally looked at my shadow self (rather than just blaming myself for being a failure) that I realized that as a child I was often denied food as a form of punishment, and rewarded with treats for good behavior. As a result I had formed a belief associating the denial of food with suffering, and eating treats with pleasure, so that every time I tried dieting as an adult, I would feel punished, and when I cheated and gave myself treats, I felt love and pleasure.

Shadow-self healing is introspective work that can trigger a lot of denial, so wear or hold black obsidian and onyx to help bring what you need to see to the surface of your awareness, and chrysoprase, rhodochrosite, and mangano calcite so that you can heal what you need to with love.

RESISTANCE AND EXCUSES: Resistance and excuses hold us back from achieving our potential, and keep us from making positive changes or choices in our lives. If you're finally willing to admit to and deal with your resistance, wear sodalite, hematite, onyx, rubellite, and nuummite daily for loving commitment and self-mastery, and to support you in being honest with yourself when you're making excuses.

....

TRUTH: You have to be honest with yourself if you want to shift, heal, or let go of what's no longer serving you. Wear amazonite, aquamarine, rose quartz, and ruby daily, or hold them while in meditation or journaling, for the loving courage, grace, and self-awareness to recognize and own your truth.

BALANCE

I love it when clients come to see me saying that they're seeking "balance." I always ask them: "What does that mean to you?" They inevitably respond: "Feeling okay." And I ask, "And what does 'okay' mean to you?"

"Well, I don't know . . . I guess it means not feeling so stressed about work, afraid of losing my job, angry at my husband, frustrated that I can't lose weight, and worried that I'll be too old to have kids when we're finally ready. I wish my mind could just be at peace for even five seconds. I'd also love it if I could sleep better," they say.

"Balance" and "okay" mean a lot of different things to different people. For some it's feeling secure, or good about themselves, or calm, or grounded, or optimistic, or healthy. There are many things that can throw us off balance, like shock or conflict, a period of ill health, stress, sadness, or anxiety. It may be about being able to navigate smoothly through rough waters, or enjoying smooth sailing without worrying about what could potentially go wrong.

Many people assume that in order to achieve balance you need to experience the opposite of whatever you're feeling, so, for instance, if you're anxious, you need to work with a crystal that will help you feel calm. For the most part this is true, but if a persistent feeling that something is wrong still lingers, it may only be temporary. If you're working with a crystal purely to address the feeling without also addressing its cause, you may find that your relief is limited, or that the crystal stops working for you altogether. If this happens, it could be a sign that you need to work with a crystal that supports you in responding to whatever's throwing you off, in a way that is loving, empowered, and consistent, not just as a quick fix for uncomfortable feelings.

So if you're anxious, angelite will help you feel calmer by quieting the mind, but then you may want to hold sodalite or amazonite and ask yourself, "What's causing my anxiety?" Maybe you'll realize that you forgot to turn the oven off, or that someone said something to you that made you feel uncomfortable and you need to talk to him about it, or that something about a deal you've been offered doesn't add up or feel right. Working with crystals can help our emotions inform us, rather than just affect us.

CRYSTAL COMBINATIONS

ANGER: Hold amethyst, rose quartz, angelite, chrysocolla, or celestite to cool anger and bring your temper back in check, or wear one of these crystals daily for temperance.

ANXIETY: See "Mind Power" on page 131.

CALM: Hold, meditate, wear, or sleep with blue lace agate, aquamarine, angelite, lithium quartz, rose quartz, ruby in fuschite, smoky quartz, black tourmaline, hematite, selenite, amethyst, or blue calcite for an overall sense of calm. You can also place a large piece or two of any these crystals in a space where you'd like to create a calming atmosphere. If you're seeking to remain calm during intense or demanding situations, for which you will also need to be focused and alert, wear blue lace agate and blue or purple fluorite, and also hematite for grounding.

DEALING WITH OVERWHELMING EMOTIONS: It seems that all of us have more and more to do, manage, and handle. Feeling overwhelmed may be debilitating because it can cause you to feel distressed, uncertain as to how to proceed, and stall you when you need to be productive. For rapid relief when hit with overwhelming emotions, grab hold of blue lace agate in your receptive hand and just breathe for a few minutes to calm the mind and subdue the feelings. To manage overwhelming emotions when faced with handling distressing situations or circumstances, wear or meditate with fuschite to help ground your energy in your heart center, so that you feel more empowered and capable of dealing with the overwhelming situation. If you're struggling to manage day-to-day tasks or have a massive workload to organize and plow through, you can wear hematite, fuschite, and blue sapphire to feel grounded, together, and focused on priorities.

FEAR: There are two kinds of fear—legitimate and illusory. If you're in the jungle and a tiger is about to pounce on you, feeling afraid is pretty legit; you're facing a real and imminent threat to your safety and well-being. When you're afraid of what might happen, or you harbor doubts and worries that exist only in your mind, then your fears are illusory. They are not real and imminent threats to your safety and well-being, and even if they do become reality, until then you are responding emotionally to something that only exists in your imagination. Fear is a natural part of the human condition—there's no getting away from it. It's how we respond to fear that counts: either with love, courage, and grace, or by freaking out and letting it eat away at our psyche.

Wear, hold, or meditate daily with two of the following to help you respond to your fear with courage, and to help keep fearful thinking at bay: blue lace agate, danburite, spirit quartz, tiger iron, black tourmaline, aqua aura quartz, aragonite star cluster, rose quartz, sugilite, celestite, red jasper, onyx, ruby, or hematite.

MOOD SWINGS: Dramatic shifts in mood or temperament are always a sign of imbalance. That imbalance may be hormonal or chemical, or stress-, spirit-, or chakra-related. Wear or meditate daily with orange calcite, carnelian, tiger eye, bloodstone, or rainbow obsidian to help gently moderate this imbalance while you seek out its cause. Making a crystal tonic of any one of these crystals can also be beneficial, but not for long-term use, as it will eventually become ineffective if you're not simultaneously addressing the cause.

RELAXATION: Basically anything pale blue, pink, lavender, white, or pale green in the crystal kingdom will have a relaxing effect on the system. My top favorites are angelite, moonstone, pink opal, blue calcite, lepidolite, rose quartz, jade, and black tourmaline. You can hold, meditate, sleep with, or wear any of these crystals as needed, or wear one daily for soothing. If you're seeking to remain relaxed during intense or demanding situations where you will also need to be focused and alert, wear blue lace agate, blue or purple fluorite, and hematite for grounding.

SHOCK: Hold ruby in fuschite, blue calcite, or lithium quartz in response to shock for as long as needed.

STAGE FRIGHT: Wear or hold hematite and carnelian if you suffer from stage fright, or are afraid of making business presentations. It helps to keep you grounded, present, and connected to your body, so that you're more in control of your breathing, thoughts, and emotions.

STRESS: Managing stress has pretty much become part of everyone's daily life. Chronic stress can lead to illness, and I've found that it's the greatest contributing factor to most energy imbalances. Ideally, the best way to ease stress is to resolve or remove the stressor from your life, but unfortunately there's a certain measure of stress with which most of us simply have to cope these days. Wearing one or two of the following crystals on a daily basis can help you manage and cope with everyday stressors: smoky quartz, blue lace agate, black tourmaline, moonstone, apophyllite, sugilite, amethyst, rose quartz, orange calcite, blue calcite, jet, lithium quartz, or angelite. To help you get through periods of intense stress, meditate regularly with angelite, tourmaline quartz, or ruby in your receptive hand, and healer's gold, black tourmaline, or smoky quartz in your dominant hand for 5–30 minutes. To clear stress from your system at the end of the day, sit and hold selenite in your receptive hand and black tourmaline or smoky quartz in your dominant hand for 20 minutes. You can also sleep with tourmaline quartz under your pillow at night.

TRANSITIONS: Big changes, like moving, going to a new job or a new school, marriage, retirement, losing your job, divorce, and other upheavals, can cause feelings of angst, fear, and disorientation. I highly recommend wearing honey calcite during these times, as it helps us to navigate change with a measure of confidence and grace, as well as helping us surrender to changes that we might be resisting or find daunting. You can pair it with other balancing crystals as needed. Other options include chrysoprase, ruby, jade, blue lace agate, tiger eye, and rainbow obsidian. It's best to wear whichever transition crystal or combination you choose daily until you feel more secure and grounded in your new circumstances.

EMPOWERMENT

I define "empowerment" as the process of reclaiming and/or exercising your personal power in accordance with your own free will, and making choices based on your own authentic desires. We cede our power to many things: authority figures, governing bodies, rules and regulations, fears, perceived obligations, other people's demands and expectations, limiting beliefs, domineering in-laws, and so on. Many of us are brought up to follow the rules, do what we're told, play it safe, fit in, make our parents proud, be quiet, and please others or we'll be punished, and we won't be loved, worthy, accepted, or safe. When we're kids, it is what it is: We don't have much choice in the matter. But when we're adults, we do. Some people go their whole lives without challenging this approach, and that's okay; we're all allowed to pursue our own process of self-actualization. But if you want more for yourself and your life, if you want to become something greater, make real and lasting change, or stand up to the schoolyard bully, at some point you are going to have to engage in the process of empowerment.

In most cases when my clients seek to either heal or change their lives, empowerment figures prominently in the process. Reclaiming my power has also been a big part of my own healing story. The great thing about working with crystals for empowerment is that you can get a daily, consistent dose of energy that can support you by amplifying your own sense of personal power, and creating greater inner awareness of when, where, and how you give your power away.

Petra was about to go through a major life change: She had started an affair with a man she dearly loved, and wanted to leave her husband for this man. It was a highly stressful time for her because she had been dependent on and bullied by her husband for years, to the point where she had no say in any matter, had no idea about the state of their finances, and was even often told how to dress. She still cared for her husband, but she had been so unhappy for so long that she just couldn't stand to remain in the marriage. Yet she was terrified of leaving because of how he might respond. Her new relationship was very different, and gave her hope that she could have a better future with someone, but she needed the courage to take the steps that were necessary for her to be free.

Our crystal work focused on stress relief, grounding, empowerment, self-worth, and intuition, so that she could develop greater trust in her own ability to make decisions, have the strength to carry them out, and feel grounded in the belief that she deserved and could have more. The process took a few months. First she began to feel less timid, then she began to think more strategically, then she got angry, and then she got strong. She retained a lawyer, found a friend to stay with, and then asked her husband for a divorce.

Her husband was furious, insisted on couples counseling, and Petra began to wobble. She asked me for a crystal combination to help her stay strong, so we put together the combination of tiger eye, ruby, hematite, blue kyanite, and sodalite for grounding, empowering, and unwavering energy that would also help her recognize her ingrained patterns of giving in to her husband's demands. She was finally able to serve him with papers, and a lengthy and nasty divorce ensued, but eventually an agreement was reached and the marriage was dissolved. Petra is now able to pursue her new relationship out in the open, and is building a successful career in interior design. She says she still wears her empowerment combo on a daily basis, since she doesn't feel she could have made it through such an ordeal without her crystal support.

CRYSTAL COMBINATIONS

BOUNDARIES: Meditate regularly, holding amazonite in your receptive hand and sunstone in your dominant hand, to support you in cultivating greater awareness of your feelings and your bottom lines, and to help empower you in honoring them. You can also wear a daily combination of sunstone, ruby, red jasper, carnelian, and green aventurine for support or to help maintain the boundaries you've established.

CONFIDENCE: Meditate regularly, holding citrine in your receptive hand and pyrite in your dominant hand for 5–15 minutes, or wear chrysoprase, ocean jasper, citrine, aragonite star cluster, and ruby on a daily basis to feel more confident. You can also make a crystal tonic from this combination for more long-term support.

COURAGE: Being brave is different from being strong. I often see people who feel that they're being strong when they're merely denying how they're feeling, and I've seen true courage when people admit their fear but are willing to take action in the face of that fear. To me, the firefighters of the FDNY who ran into World Trade Center Tower 1 after Tower 2 collapsed on 9/11, knowing that they were risking a similar fate but determined to do their duty, exemplified a tremendous act of courage. Wear spirit quartz, bloodstone, red jasper, ruby, pyrite, aquamarine, or tiger iron for courage, or hold one of these when you feel you most need it.

DETERMINATION: Grab hold of onyx, tiger iron, and red jasper, or wear them when needed, to bolster and secure your sense of determination.

EMPOWERED CHOICES: Wear ruby and emerald daily when you've decided to live a more empowered, heart-centered life. Remember that your choices determine your destiny. The more you make authentic choices based on your true desires, the better and more fulfilling your life will be.

INDEPENDENCE: Wear hematite, rose quartz, azurite, and ruby when you're working toward a greater sense or state of independence.

LEADERSHIP: Become the leading lady or man in your story by wearing aragonite star cluster, ruby, and eudialyte daily, which helps you tap into your true strength and nobility.

SPEAKING UP: Afraid of speaking up or being heard? Your voice is a big part of your personal power, so it needs to be open, strong, and authentic, but this can take courage. Wear aquamarine for courage; blue lace agate for a calm, steady voice; blue kyanite to articulate your thoughts more clearly; amazonite to support you in speaking your truth; aqua aura quartz when you're standing up for yourself; or chrysocolla when you want to be able to speak with more compassion.

STEADFASTNESS: Hold a piece of hematite in each hand when facing a conflict, confrontation, or negotiation where you will need to hold your power and stand your ground. You can also wear black tourmaline, tiger iron, and ruby on a daily basis when you wish to remain steadfast in your intentions, decisions, and boundaries.

FORGIVENESS

Derrick was a highly successful dancer for a world-renowned company in New York City. He started working with me after ending what he had thought was a monogamous relationship with a man who had cheated on him and infected him with HIV. Derrick was seething with rage and vengeful thoughts toward his ex, he felt deeply hurt and betrayed, and on top of feeling that he had "been handed a death sentence," he was very worried that he would lose muscle mass and would no longer be able to dance. He was consumed with hating his ex, wishing him harm, going over and over scenarios in his head, so that he was working himself into a constant state of heightened emotion, anger, worry, and stress. We had a number of things to address—stress, emotional wounding, health, and vitality—but I finally said to him, "Derrick, while your feelings are valid and understandable, they're going to eat you alive if you don't start letting them go."

He had a lot to forgive—not just his ex-boyfriend, but also his own feelings of shame, anger, and poor judgment for having trusted that man and having jeopardized his life and his career. Forgiveness is a process; it doesn't just happen overnight. But with the right crystals we can work on finding acceptance, compassion, and ultimately peace with any situation, no matter how terrible or traumatic. It's important to note that in the act of forgiveness we are not condoning the actions or behavior of another; we are merely freeing ourselves from the ties that bind us to our painful pasts. Slowly, over time, Derrick moved forward in peace, and kept his energy focused on staying well and pursuing his passion and his art.

CRYSTAL COMBINATIONS

ACCEPTANCE: If you're still in a place where you wish something (or someone) hadn't happened to you, or that things had been different, you are not in a place of acceptance. When you're able to accept that what happened happened, you'll be better prepared to move on. Wear, sleep, or meditate daily with mangano calcite, rose quartz, amethyst, and apache tear to help support you in shifting into a place of acceptance.

ANGER (RELEASING): It's important to acknowledge and give vent to your anger before you can move on to acceptance. Some people find this easy, but others try (rather unsuccessfully) to skip this step and move straight on to compassion and forgiveness. As long as you harbor anger, you can't move forward, because anger demands to be acknowledged and released. I had a teacher once who often said that "anger is loud hurt." You can't heal if you keep hurting. You can wear or hold black obsidian, rhodochrosite, and blue kyanite to get in touch with your anger and give it voice in a way that won't do harm to yourself or anyone else. Some safe ways of channeling and releasing anger include writing letters that you tear up and burn, punching pillows, screaming while under water, painting, or drawing.

COMPASSION: Love is the answer, but sometimes that can be very hard to muster for those we have to forgive, even if the one we need to forgive is ourself. Being able to feel compassion for someone who's wronged us can seem like too much to ask, and yet if we truly want to heal, we must. Wearing this combo daily in a pouch over your heart chakra can help support you in this process: pink kunzite, jade, watermelon tourmaline, emerald, and rainbow obsidian. You can also make a crystal tonic from this combination, especially if you need this to be a gentle, sensitive, and gradual process.

MAKING AMENDS: Acknowledging and apologizing for a mistake may be daunting, but it's necessary for personal growth and the development of a greater quality of life and a stronger character. Work regularly with chrysoprase, apache tear, septarian, snowflake obsidian, and aragonite star cluster by wearing them, sleeping with them, or making a tonic of them, to help you cultivate the humility, conviction, and courage to honor this process.

PEACE: Sleep with selenite and moonstone under your pillow, or have large pieces by your bedside, to support you in ushering in a sense of peace and closure when you feel that you have resolved and come to terms with a situation.

MIND POWER

The power of the mind is paramount. When your mind is your ally, there's very little you can't achieve; when it's working against you, it can be your greatest enemy. Our minds have a lot to manage these days: stress, uncertainty and fear, overwork, multitasking, increased demands, sleep deficits, health issues, and overstimulation. Everything is moving faster and faster. Mental health is a growing issue; with the lack of access to good mental health care, and limited understanding or negative stigmas associated with mental health, a lot of people are suffering without enough help and support.

Crystals work well in conjunction with traditional treatments for mental health issues, or they can provide a natural, holistic alternative if you're unwilling to use medications. You can work with crystal energy to help you retrain your brain to work for you, instead of against you.

Marisol was working with me to help her pass her nursing exam, which she had failed twice already. She was very worried that she would fail the exam a third time, so we were working with crystals in her healing sessions to help her manage her anxiety and stress effectively, increase her ability to focus, improve her memory, and shore up her confidence. Her goal was to finally pass the exam and move on to a better and brighter future. Marisol would leave our sessions feeling upbeat and optimistic, and would find that her ability to study and focus had improved, but then she would start dwelling on her failures, her weaknesses, and her fears, and she'd lose hope. Her ingrained negative patterns of thought and her inner critic were beating her down and holding her back. Her mind was behaving like her own worst enemy.

We switched tacks, and while we were still addressing her anxieties and strengthening her cognitive abilities, we also started working with crystals to affect her subconscious and shift her self-defeating mentality to positive and empowering thought patterns. Later that week Marisol had a breakthrough: A few nights before the exam, she was studying, when all of a sudden her inner critic started in on her about how she was kidding herself, that she'd never make it, and filling her mind with visions of getting another big red "F" on her exam paper. Something snapped, and Marisol physically stood up and told that voice out loud that she was tired of hearing it, she didn't believe in it anymore, and that she was determined to succeed. She then pictured an image of the "F" being crossed out and switched to an "A." The voice went silent, and each time it surfaced, Marisol stood up to it and then shifted the vision. Days later she took that exam, still nervous but determined to succeed, and while she didn't score an "A," she was overjoyed to find that she had received a passing grade. Her greatest achievement, however, was in learning how to make her mind her ally in working toward achieving her dreams, rather than in letting her fears overwhelm her.

CRYSTAL COMBINATIONS

ANXIETY: While anxiety is something we experience as a feeling, its root is mental. When you're able to discover the source of your disquiet and take action to address it, or redirect the energy of anxiety into affirmative, empowered thinking, anxiety typically dissolves. For example, if your anxiety is springing from having a list of more tasks and obligations than you can manage, you can take steps to delegate, automate, or edit that list. If not yet knowing the results from a health test is causing you anxiety, you can meditate or wear a soothing crystal to help quiet fearful thoughts and alleviate the feelings. My favorite go-to crystals for anxiety are lithium quartz, followed by angelite, because they're fast-acting and help me to create the mental space I need to get in tune with what's bothering me so that I can then choose how to respond.

Holding any one of the following crystals for 5–10 minutes in your receptive hand will help to ease feelings of anxiety: amethyst, blue lace agate, lithium quartz, rose quartz, angelite, rainbow obsidian, or lepidolite. Meditating or sleeping with any one or two of these crystals can also be of great benefit. If you want to wear an anxiety-easing crystal throughout the day, stick with either amethyst, blue lace agate, rose quartz, and/or rainbow obsidian, as they'll help you to manage the energy without any detrimental impact on your alertness or other cognitive functions. Lithium quartz and angelite may prompt feelings of deep relaxation or mellowness, which may not be beneficial to you if, say, you're taking an exam, driving, or in contract negotiations, where you need to focus on the task at hand.

CLARITY: Wear or hold onyx, fluorite, blue sapphire, citrine, blue kyanite, tourmaline quartz, or clear quartz when you desire clarity of thought, vision, or understanding. Be careful if you choose to wear clear quartz throughout the day, as it may amplify and/or magnify other feelings or states of being that may or may not be beneficial at that point.

COGNITIVE FUNCTION: Wear or hold blue sapphire, blue kyanite, fluorite, aragonite star cluster, red jasper, or sodalite to improve learning, thinking, memory, reasoning, deduction, strategic thinking, the articulation or presentation of ideas, problem solving, prioritizing, and/or organizing activities.

CREATIVE THINKING AND TROUBLESHOOTING: When you feel the need to think outside the box a little more, come up with new ideas, solve problems, create a vision that is new or inspired, or figure out why something's not working (like a broken toaster) and how to fix it, meditate on it while holding optical calcite, fluorite, and azurite, or lie down with the azurite in your receptive hand, fluorite in your dominant hand, and optical calcite on your third eye chakra. The fluorite and azurite help to expand your thinking, while the optical calcite aides in shifting your perspective. As an alternative, you can also wear them throughout the day, but in this case meditation is best as it helps to quiet the mind and create space for ideas to come through.

DEPRESSION: Meditate daily with citrine and amethyst for 20–40 minutes. You can also wear citrine, amethyst, rubellite, ocean jasper, and sunstone throughout the day, or make a crystal tonic from this combination to be taken 3–5 times daily. Sleep with rose quartz and black tourmaline at night. To discover the source or cause of your depression, meditate on it while holding labradorite in your receptive hand and apache tear in your dominant hand.

FOCUS: Wear fluorite, rhodonite, blue sapphire, tiger iron, and blue kyanite to stay sharp, focused, and on point. If your focus requires a certain measure of determination, or if it's being significantly challenged by distractions, substitute the rhodonite for onyx.

MEMORY ISSUES: If you find that you're being particularly forgetful lately, or are experiencing memory loss or blocked memories, meditate or make a crystal tonic with fluorite, black obsidian, and Herkimer diamond. You can wear this combination on a daily basis to improve memory function, but if you are working to unblock memories (that could potentially be traumatic), use it only when in a therapeutic environment.

....

MENTAL STRESS: If your mind keeps turning back to something that's stressing you out, or you're causing yourself stress by overthinking or overanalyzing, or you're putting yourself under too much pressure, grab hold of amethyst and angelite to give yourself a bit of a mental break. They help to calm the mind and give you the energy to pull out of stressful thinking patterns. For daily maintenance, you can wear or make a crystal tonic from the following combination: smoky quartz, blue calcite, amethyst, honey calcite, and rainbow obsidian. You can also sleep with angelite, rose quartz, and lepidolite under your pillow at night.

....

NEGATIVE THOUGHT PATTERNS: These are thoughts, voices in your head, or limiting beliefs that exist in your subconscious and talk you down ("You're so uncool"), talk you out of things ("You're too old to try that now, so don't bother"), or dictate and limit your choices ("You'll never find an apartment you can afford in that area, so you're stuck in this crappy neighborhood" or "Life is suffering"). When we give power to these patterns and let them rule us, we get in our own way, block our potential, settle for low expectations and results, and make ourselves miserable. Wear amethyst, hematite, citrine, azurite, and rubellite daily to have a positive influence on the subconscious, helping you to consciously rework, break, or shift your negative patterns of thought. You can also meditate regularly holding a piece of chrysanthemum stone in both hands for 15–30 minutes.

WORRY AND APPREHENSION: Wear aquamarine, blue calcite, and amethyst to soothe anticipatory stress and anxiety, while bolstering your sense of courage, so that you can calmly face what's coming, and to shift your attention away from your worries.

OWNING YOUR LIGHT

The mistake a lot of people make in their healing process is focusing exclusively on what they want to heal, release, or change, and not paying enough attention to their strengths, talents, and blessings. In many cases I've found that putting more energy and focus on our light actually trumps or dissolves a lot of what was plaguing us in our shadow. You can bring a candle into a darkened room, but you can't bring darkness into light; it simply disappears. Certainly we need to heal and resolve what might be blocking us or holding us back, but on the path to self-actualization, which means reaching our full potential, our light qualities are essential.

Everyone is good at something, everyone has something to offer; each and every one of us has an attractive quality, dreams that we can achieve, power and abilities we can cultivate, love we can share, and the possibility of joy. Every single person has a purpose for being here, a reason to exist, and value in the Universe. When we take time to discover and nurture all the great things about ourselves, we start to feel better, more confident, more fulfilled, more capable, and more worthy. We're less likely to let things get us down, or we bounce back more quickly. We're less likely to cede our power, and we're more likely to go for what we want and to celebrate ourselves. We're more likely to discover and pursue our dreams, and less likely to settle for what doesn't feel right or make us happy.

I have a client who's a gifted screenwriter. When she first came to see me, she was a down-and-out actress earning a living as a personal assistant. She was very stressed, unhappy, anxious, insecure, and frequently fell ill with one type of ailment or another. One day she mentioned to me that every time her acting career started to take off she would get sick, so I suggested to her that perhaps her body was telling her to do something else. She confessed that she loved to write and harbored a secret desire to become a screenwriter, but she feared she'd never be good enough or succeed at it. Who was she to put her ideas and stories out there into the world? How could she possibly stack up against all the great writers whom she admired?

I suggested she try, and we worked with crystals to help empower her, spark her creative drive and passions, and boost her confidence, self-worth, and faith, giving her "crystal tune-ups" whenever she started to feel blocked, resistant, or stressed. She started with a short series of sketches that reflected her quirky, irreverent sense of humor and love for awkward people and situations, channeling her feelings about herself and stories she'd always wanted to tell into her scripts. She then filmed them and launched them online. Even though she was fearful of rejection and criticism, she took a deep breath and emailed all her friends and colleagues, inviting them to watch the series and give her feedback. To her great delight and surprise, she got great reviews. The series developed a following, and she is now happily pursuing new and rewarding projects. She made a choice to own and embrace her light and it paid off!

CRYSTAL COMBINATIONS

AMBITION: If your "get up and go" got up and went without you, meditate daily with garnet in your receptive hand and pyrite in your dominant hand, or wear pyrite, citrine, and garnet daily to rev up your ambition.

CELEBRATION: Wear septarian, rose quartz, citrine, and chrysoprase to help shift your perspective to all the good and wonderful things about yourself and your life.

GRATITUDE: Resentment, poverty mentality, pessimism, and cynicism drain your energy, bring you down, and significantly limit your options. If you find that you're getting caught in this headspace and want to pull out of it, or if you're seeking to cultivate a greater sense of gratitude for yourself, wear rhodonite, chrysoprase, citrine, septarian, and green aventurine, or make a crystal tonic of this combination, to feel more genuine gratitude. You can also meditate regularly with jade in your receptive hand and rose quartz in your dominant hand.

HAPPINESS: Happiness is a choice—I've witnessed people in some of the most desperate and dire circumstances still making the genuine choice to find something to be happy about. I freely admit that I've had to make this a conscious practice, because for a while I was a very stressed-out, burned-out individual, who was more inclined to choose misery over happiness. I finally got wise to myself on this, and it's made my life so much better, and difficult or challenging times so much more bearable, as a result. Wear sunstone, ocean jasper, citrine, pink kunzite, and blue apatite to support you in feeling happy, or make a crystal tonic from this combination for an everyday, consistent lift. If you feel as if you need some help in choosing to be happy when you're feeling miserable, hold or meditate with chrysanthemum stone in your receptive hand and apophyllite in your dominant hand, which will help lift your perspective to a more Zenlike mind-set and mood.

JOY: Wear hiddenite, citrine, pink opal, and gold rutilated quartz to put yourself in a pleasurable, unruffled, and joyful mood.

MOOD LIFTER: Wear ocean jasper, citrine, rose quartz, and green aventurine to put you in a sunny, breezy mood. You can also meditate with amethyst in your receptive hand and rose quartz in your dominant hand if you're feeling really down on yourself, or down about life in general.

OPTIMISM: Wear citrine, ocean jasper, sunstone, azurite, and ruby, or make a crystal tonic of this combination and take it daily to help you adopt and maintain an optimistic outlook.

PASSION: Wear or hold carnelian, garnet, and ruby to ignite some juicy, gutsy, gorgeous passion.

PLAYFULNESS: The child within us keeps our magic, hope, and wonder alive. Our creative genius, inspired selves, and imagination come to life when we allow ourselves to let go and play. Wear pink kunzite, citrine, aqua aura quartz, and silver rutilated quartz to tap into your childlike wellsprings of joy.

PLEASURE: If you're feeling unenthusiastic or blocked in your ability to enjoy pleasure (in every and any form), meditating daily with orange calcite in your receptive hand and carnelian in your dominant hand, or wearing garnet, ruby, pink aventurine, amazonite, and sunstone, can help to dissolve this block and stimulate greater enthusiasm for life, ability to experience pleasure, and enjoyment of your own feelings.

WARMTH: You know that person who lights up a room, who always seeks to make someone feel welcome, who's willing to listen without prejudice, or with whom you always feel loved and comfortable? There's a certain giving quality to her love, compassion, joy, and exuberance for life that I characterize as warmth. Wear citrine, watermelon tourmaline, garnet, and mookaite jasper when you want to be that person.

CHAPTER

8

Spirituality

BUILT MY HEALING PRACTICE helping people with their health and their lives. But I was first drawn to crystals years before that for their spiritual elements, and I've had many seekers work with me since then to expand their spiritual selves, to activate and strengthen their psychic abilities, or to experience altered and transcendent states. I've said this to students of mine over and over again: Psychic phenomena are the easy stuff when it comes to crystals; it's healing that requires more work and dedication. Tapping into our hidden or dormant gifts is a specialty of crystals, and I believe that working with crystals is the most powerful and user-friendly way to do so. I often tell my clients that increased intuition, more lively dream states, and more acute senses will be natural by-products of working with me, and I've seldom been wrong.

Simone first started working with me to help her manage the stress and nervousness she experienced while on the set of her prime-time TV show. As she became more grounded and centered in her life, her curiosity about crystals and spirituality blossomed. She was interested in growing spiritually and developing more of that side of herself. We began work on strengthening her third eye chakra (intuition, psychic ability) with crystals like amethyst, sugilite, Herkimer diamond, and azurite, and also expanding her crown chakra (access to wisdom, higher guidance, and the Divine) with selenite, danburite, and moonstone. She had a fascination with angels, and at the start of a session I saw the energy of two angels coalesce in the room. I mentioned this to her, and she burst into ecstatic tears because she had felt their presence, and had just thought to herself, "There are angels in here." She couldn't believe that I had picked up on it, too, and it was confirmation for her that not only did she have divine guidance and presence in her life, but that she could trust in her ability to sense it. She chose to cultivate this connection, and she tells me that she now regularly checks in with her angels before making any major decisions, when she needs comforting or healing, or even when she needs to find a parking space! She says she can't imagine her life without these guardians by her side, and is grateful that crystals helped her to develop and trust the ability to sense them.

Damon was going into business with someone he didn't trust. The opportunity felt like a golden one, and his sense was that it would be lucrative, but he also knew he'd have to be very strategic and watch his back along the way. He came to see me because he was seeking every edge in this relationship; he wanted to significantly sharpen his intuition, and be able to "read" what his business partner was thinking, anticipating her moves before she made them. I explained to him that reading another person's thoughts is a violation of her free will, so I wouldn't go there. But we could work on developing his clairsentience so that he could sense whether she was lying or being manipulative, bolstering his claircognizance so that he could receive divine guidance and have a stronger sense of knowing things in advance, and sharpening his intuition so that he could make the right moves at the right time while trusting his instincts. We worked regularly with tiger eye and honey calcite for clairsentience, selenite and blue kyanite for claircognizance, amethyst and Herkimer diamond for intuition, and shiva lingam to anchor all this energy in his body, so that he could trust and follow what was coming to him more easily. The business did generate a lot of money, but it was also a toxic mess, with Damon and his business partner constantly at odds with each other. Part of the guidance Damon was consistently receiving was that he deserved to be in a healthier situation, and that he could be more successful if he branched out on his own.

Finally, he took the leap of faith and followed his guidance step by step. He now brokers major commercial and corporate real estate listings in Manhattan, and credits his extrasensory perception as well as his work with crystals as a big part of his success.

AURAS AND ENERGY CLEARING

Living in New York City (which is the energetic equivalent of a pressure cooker) and doing spiritual work for a living, I was constantly engaging with other people's energy, stress, emotional baggage, and psychic debris. Given that I'm a sensitive and highly empathic individual, I became quite militant about shielding my aura and clearing my energy; otherwise, I was prone to becoming overwhelmed and even sick. The aura is an energy field that emanates around us, and yet it is intrinsically connected and integrated with our other energy systems, including our chakras and our subtle bodies (the etheric structures and blueprints of our physical body, thoughts, feelings, and soul), and impacts our physical, mental, emotional, and spiritual health and well-being.

It's important to keep your aura and energy clear (meaning free of psychic debris, lower energy vibrations, pathogens, and unhealthy attachments) to maintain your health and energy balance, and to encourage the flow of healing energy throughout your system. We can easily pick up unwanted or imbalanced energy from people, places, and even objects. It can adhere to our energy just like a string or a bit of fluff will cling to a television screen when it's turned off; hence the term "psychic debris." When this happens, we may start to feel drained, and experience body aches, mood swings, symptoms of illness, nightmares, and restless or disturbed sleep. We may stop feeling or behaving like ourselves. I like to describe it as feeling weighed down, as if we were covered in several layers of blankets, and experiencing anxiety, irritation, depression, or anger with no apparent cause, or a sense of being threatened by irrational fears and worries.

You can work with one or two of the crystals listed below to clear your aura and energy system. Choose whichever options are most practical and enjoyable for you, and bear in mind that, in order for them to be effective, the crystals need to be at least the size of a deck of playing cards, approximately 3"/7.5cm in diameter. Aura clearing is best practiced on a daily basis. Also see Chapter 10, "Crystal Healing Baths," on page 201.

CRYSTAL COMBINATIONS

BLACK TOURMALINE AND SELENITE: Hold a piece of black tourmaline in your dominant hand and a piece of selenite in your receptive hand while meditating for 20–45 minutes. You can also do this while watching TV, on the phone, on the bus, and the like.

....

HEALER'S GOLD: Sleep with healer's gold at night, or make a crystal tonic from its energy to help clear, restore, and strengthen your aura.

....

SELENITE STICK: Pass a selenite stick (at least 9"/22.5cm long) down all four sides of your body (including over your head and under your arms) and then under both your feet. You can also place a flat piece of selenite under your pillow, or sleep holding a selenite stick at night.

AURA HEALING

The aura can become damaged in a number of ways, including but not limited to: high stress or ill health, shock or trauma, psychic attack, etheric attachments, and heavy drug or alcohol use. Imagine Swiss cheese, or a paper-thin sheet of ice that can easily crack or break. That's what a damaged aura often looks and feels like.

When the aura is damaged, you're much more vulnerable to the effects of lower, harmful energy. Symptoms of a damaged aura include: fatigue, exhaustion, or feelings of overall weakness; catching colds one after the other; heightened sensitivity; being easily influenced or manipulated by others; disturbing dreams or nightmares; mental and emotional imbalances; and social neediness or a fear of being alone.

Wear infinite, spirit quartz, bloodstone, ajoite, and elestial quartz for a full day, including sleeping with them at night as comfortably as you can. It's best to do this on a day of rest, drinking plenty of water and eating fresh, vital, cooked foods that are easy to digest, so that your system can divert as much of its energy as possible to healing. Afterwards, maintain a regular energy clearing and aura shielding practice (see "Protection" on page 172).

SMOKY QUARTZ: Hold this in your receptive hand while meditating or relaxing for 40–60 minutes, place it at your feet while sleeping at night, or wear a smaller piece daily as a preventive measure.

....

SPIRIT QUARTZ: Also known as cactus quartz or fairy quartz, wear or hold this in your receptive hand for 30–45 minutes, or place a larger specimen (approximately 5"–6"/12.5–15cm) by your bedside.

....

TOURMALINE QUARTZ: Meditate with tourmaline quartz for 25–40 minutes or place it under your pillow at night.

AWAKENING AND EXPANDING CONSCIOUSNESS

You are not your thoughts; you are your soul. "Consciousness" can mean different things, depending on the beliefs and philosophy you espouse, but for me and within the scope of this book, it means becoming aware of the fact that we are more than just our daily routines, obligations, and thoughts. We are part of a greater whole, intimately connected to and a reflection of an infinite Universe of diverse realities, dimensions, levels of experience, and beings. Or, in simpler terms, that there's more out there, and more to life, than what we feel or think we're limited to, and that we are far more powerful than we could ever imagine. It's not something that can be easily explained; it's more experiential, like brief moments of bliss, periods of enlightenment, those stunning moments where we fully merge into an awareness that's beyond our regular experience.

I had an experience once meditating with sugilite. I was lying down on my bed and had placed it on my third eye chakra, with a

EMPATHS

If you're an empath—meaning that your sensitivity to emotional energy is so heightened that not only are you easily influenced by the feelings of other people, but you also have a tendency to absorb those feelings like a sponge—you require a little extra loving care. Empaths typically absorb energy first in their solar plexus chakra, where the psychic ability of clairsentience is located. As the absorption builds up, their will, ability to manifest, vital energy, personal power, and digestion can become sluggish and blocked. Place malachite on your solar plexus to draw out the blockage, and hold selenite in your receptive hand for purifying energy, while placing smoky quartz at the bottom of your dominant foot to pull that energy down and out of the body. Do this for 30–45 minutes as needed.

mere 5 minutes to meditate before I had to leave for an appointment. Suddenly, I was surrounded by golden light, floating in a pool of gold in the middle of what looked like the sun. I felt connected to the whole Universe, all knowledge, but beyond knowledge, and beyond my earthly experience, or even the identity of being me. I just was. It was warm, safe; it was an experience of bliss. It felt like an hour, and then my alarm went off to signal that my 5 minutes were up. I will never forget those 5 minutes for as long as I live. That experience of expansiveness and "all one" allowed me to grasp those concepts in a much more real way, and opened the door to greater levels of spiritual experience, awareness, and gratitude.

The important thing to remember is that awakening and expanding consciousness is not something that you can force; it's something that you have to allow and be open to experiencing. Oftentimes, people have reported falling asleep while doing this work. If that happens to you, it's okay. It's still working. It just means that your system has to adjust to the higher levels of frequencies and crystal vibrations running through your body and is knocking you out in the process. Keep persisting, and try balancing the vibrations by holding a piece of smoky quartz or jet in your dominant hand for grounding while doing this work. It's very important to ground yourself after this work by either holding a grounding stone (see "Grounding" on page 162), going for a leisurely walk, or eating.

CRYSTAL COMBINATIONS

AWAKENING CONSCIOUSNESS: Lie down comfortably and place a ¾"/2cm piece of sugilite on your third eye chakra, or place a 1½"/3.8cm piece on your heart chakra, while holding danburite in your receptive hand for expansiveness and elestial quartz in your dominant hand to help balance the energy. You can also place a 1½"/3.8cm piece of selenite at your crown chakra, and, if you feel you need additional anchoring within your body (so that you don't panic if you feel like you're losing control), a 2"/5cm piece of smoky quartz on your root chakra, or 1"/2.5cm pieces of smoky quartz at each foot. Do not do this for more than one hour.

CLEARING A BLOCKED CROWN CHAKRA: If you feel blocked or if you keep forcing the process, place clear calcite on your pillow at the top of your crown chakra and sleep with it at night, or meditate daily with it in your receptive hand and elestial quartz in your dominant hand for 20 minutes. Clear calcite helps to gently clear and expand the crown chakra, supporting us in surrendering to the flow of the Universe, while the elestial quartz helps draw greater amounts of light down into our energy system.

CONSCIOUS AWARENESS: I also like to think of "consciousness" as living with greater intention, attention, purpose, awareness, respect, and gratitude. This usually requires us to slow down, appreciate, listen, practice more compassion, and be present. When people are engaging in spiritual work and practices, they sometimes struggle with a false sense of separation from their spiritual and everyday selves. Our body and soul make up our whole, dynamic, divine selves, so integrating both of those parts of ourselves and our lives is essential. Wear or meditate daily with elestial quartz to help ground your spiritual senses and experiences in your everyday existence. Over time this will make you feel more complete, whole, and integrated.

EXPANDING CONSCIOUSNESS: Meditate holding danburite in your receptive hand and apophyllite in your dominant hand, and take a few deep breaths while focusing on clearing your mind. Use your breath and awareness to keep returning to an image or feeling of open space or emptiness. Danburite propels us into higher realms of consciousness and experience, while apophyllite expands our awareness, openness, and receptivity, and frees us from being dominated by our egos. If this combination feels too strong for you, you can balance it out with a piece of smoky quartz for grounding, or try working with smaller-sized crystals.

CHANNELING, MEDIUMSHIP, AND GUIDES

If you're a channel or medium, or if you're inclined to work with guides for healing, divination, or in your everyday life, crystals can be powerful allies in your work by helping to amplify, strengthen, and clarify your connection. When doing Akashic Record readings, for instance, where I connect with the realm of the Akasha for soul-level guidance, healing, and information, I always wear danburite and apophyllite, which vibrate on the same frequency as the Akashic field (a realm of divine knowledge), and selenite, which raises my vibration so that I can receive clear, accurate, and pertinent information for my clients. This crystal combination helps to align my energy more powerfully with the realm and guides I'm seeking to access, making everything easier and smoother. As a result, I feel supported and confident while doing my work.

Working with crystals also helps ensure that the energy and guidance I'm receiving are coming from a higher, divine, and loving source. Crystals help to filter out lower, harmful, pathogenic, or dark frequencies and entities that may seek to give me inaccurate, misleading guidance and information, or that may seek to form an unhealthy energy attachment to me. For those of you new to the work, it's essential to remember that, just as there are people who can do us harm or make mischief, there are spirits that can do us harm or make mischief.

Juanita had been dabbling in channeling, mediumship, and séances, and had a powerful ability to connect and communicate with spirits. She was open to communicating with whatever presence she sensed without ever discerning if it was wise or safe for her to do so. She had started working with a spirit who would speak to her, give her bad advice, and claimed to be helping her, but actually had malicious intentions. Her friends and family began to notice a change in her: She was becoming more secretive, suspicious, short-tempered, and drained. The spirit was telling her that people were lying to her, that her family was holding her back from achieving greatness, that her friends were jealous of her. When people raised concerns about the change in her demeanor, this spirit would find ways to twist it into proof that these people were lining up against Juanita.

She began to have terrible nightmares and felt as if everything was going wrong for her. The spirit was telling her that someone was cursing her, so she came to see me in hopes that I could lift the curse. I immediately sensed that something was off, and the more I asked about this spirit who was guiding Juanita and what it was telling her, the more convinced I became that it was doing her harm. I suggested to Juanita that we do a spirit clearing, assuring her that if it was a spirit of the light her connection to it would remain, but if it was a dark spirit she would feel better almost immediately.

She did feel better right away, and Juanita steered clear of spirit communication for a while after that. Now training with a medium who knows how to do the work safely, she told me that she's learned her lesson: She will never interact with a spirit again without determining first if it's a spirit of the light. And she always carries black tourmaline for protection, just in case.

CRYSTAL COMBINATIONS

CHANNELING: Whatever method you might be using for channeling, wearing a combination of quartz, danburite, and ajoite will help you form a stronger connection, and allow the information to flow through more smoothly and clearly.

....

MEDIUMSHIP: Wear or hold selenite to keep the crown chakra open and receptive, and to raise your vibration. And wear angelite, pink kunzite, and ajoite to form a strong, clear connection, for accurate and articulate expression, and to help anchor the energy in your heart center.

....

SPIRIT FILTER: Wear elestial quartz, selenite, black tourmaline, and blue kyanite, or have several of these crystals placed in a circle around you, to help filter out any lower, harmful frequencies, spirits, or vibrations.

CRYSTALS AND SPIRITS FROM OTHER REALMS

Like radio dials and antennae, you can work with crystals to help you establish a connection and be in tune with any form of energy or frequency in the Universe, and therefore with any guide, spirit, realm, or even planet you choose.

ANGELS

Most of us have heard of angels—messengers of God ranked in higher divine orders from gentle guardians and guides to archangelic warriors and keepers of arcane knowledge. They are nondenominational emissaries who appear in numerous holy texts, religions, and faiths throughout the world.

CRYSTAL COMBINATIONS

CHANNELING ANGELIC ENERGY: If you work with angelic energy in healing, channeling, or divination work, meditate daily with scolecite and celestite, or wear these crystals during your sessions.

....

CONNECTING WITH ANGELIC ENERGY: Meditate with or hold ajoite to connect and surround yourself with angelic energy. This is excellent for times when you need healing, protection, guidance, good fortune, or forgiveness. You can also wear ajoite, but, given its high vibration, it can make you feel spaced-out, so balance its energies with smoky quartz or jet.

....

RECEIVING ANGELIC GUIDANCE: To connect with your angelic guides and to receive their communication more clearly, sleep with angelite under your pillow and wear pink kunzite daily, or meditate while holding both crystals regularly. You can also make an angelite and pink kunzite crystal tonic for the same purposes.

ANIMAL TOTEMS

Animal totems or power animals are the representative spirits of the animal kingdom, and are called on for guidance, protection, and healing, primarily in shamanic practices. But they are available to every person who calls on them or wishes to work with them. The combinations below will also support and enhance shamanic journeywork.

CRYSTAL COMBINATIONS

DISCOVERING YOUR ANIMAL TOTEM: Hold red jasper in your receptive hand and azurite in your dominant hand and meditate with the intention of seeing your animal totem in your mind's eye.

....

RECEIVING MESSAGES, GUIDANCE, OR HEALING FROM YOUR ANIMAL TOTEM: Bury a piece of clear quartz in the ground or the soil of a plant for 24 hours, then hold it in your receptive hand and black tourmaline in your dominant hand. Relax into a meditative state, visualize your totem, and make your request.

ASCENDED MASTERS

Ascended masters are great prophets, mystics, healers, and teachers, most of whom lived once in human history, and who have remained present and available in spirit form as divine guides. The Buddha, Jesus Christ, St. Germain, and Kwan Yin are all examples of ascended masters. We may seek their guidance and we may also seek to embody some of their energy, meaning that we can receive some of their energy and then be influenced by it physically, mentally, emotionally, or spiritually, just as we are with crystals.

CRYSTAL COMBINATIONS

EMBODYING ASCENDED MASTER ENERGY: Hold healer's gold while meditating on your chosen ascended master and visualizing being filled by the master's energy. Then wear it throughout your day or as needed. You can also make a crystal tonic if you are looking for a gentler, more cumulative effect over time by doing the same exercise and then following the crystal tonic guidelines in this book.

RECEIVING ASCENDED MASTER GUIDANCE: Hold selenite and apophyllite while in a meditative state when seeking to connect to and/or channel guidance from an ascended master.

ELEMENTS

Some people (myself included) like to work with the spirits of the elements. Because this is a very old, intimate, and highly diverse practice, I will simply suggest crystals that match the frequency of elements without suggesting methods of use. Let the essence of the energy itself guide you!

CRYSTALS

AIR: selenite, celestite, or clear quartz

EARTH: shiva lingam, mookaite jasper, or aragonite star cluster

FIRE: moldavite, carnelian, or sugilite

METAL: hematite, healer's gold, or bloodstone

STORM: pietersite, black obsidian, or labradorite

WATER: chrysocolla, aquamarine, or silver rutilated quartz

WOOD: moss agate, jade, or tiger eye

FAERIES

Working with faeries is tricky: They're not governed by the same moral or ethical codes as other beings, so they don't feel the need to play nice, be fair, or be helpful to you in any way. Some are certainly benevolent, but others can be downright harmful or scary. That being said, they are spirits of nature and are all around us especially when we're in natural settings, near elements of nature (like crystals, plants, water, and fire), or if we have an affinity for them. So it's nice to be able to see them or experience their energy. Wearing healer's gold while you're in their vicinity is a good idea, because it will be protective against their uninvited or unwanted influences.

CRYSTAL COMBINATIONS

COMMUNICATING WITH FAERIES: Wear staurolite or meditate with it for 30–40 minutes before making contact. This will also work for seeing through the veil into their realm.

....

FEELING FAERY ENERGY: Wear infinite or meditate with it for 15–30 minutes prior to going into nature. Making a crystal tonic of infinite and consuming it regularly will help to heighten your senses. It is also excellent for healing the aura.

....

SEEING FAERIES: Wear chiastolite or hold it while relaxing your gaze and be open to seeing shifting forms, coalescing energy, sparks of colored light, or faeries in corporeal form.

NATURE

If you're an urban dweller or spend most of your time indoors, you can miss that healing, soothing, and restorative feeling you get from nature. Having grown up in Canada, I found it necessary living in New York City to surround myself with plants, animals, and crystals as much as possible to balance out the overwhelming, energy-draining effects of the city.

Spending time in nature can dramatically reduce stress levels and the effects of stress on our health. Communing with nature can also give our system a reboot so that we have more energy and vitality throughout the day. But when you can't get away for the weekend, or even take your lunch break in the park, working with crystals can still connect you with that nature vibe.

CRYSTAL COMBINATIONS

HEALING NATURE ENERGY: Wear, meditate, or sleep with moss agate and green calcite to receive the healing vibrations of nature. Placing a large piece of infinite or spirit quartz in a room also invites benevolent nature spirits into the space.

NATURE HEALING TONIC: You can make a crystal tonic of green calcite, moss agate, and infinite to be taken daily as part of your health maintenance regimen, or during times of stress.

RESTORATIVE NATURE ENERGY: Wear or meditate with shiva lingam and infinite to revitalize and replenish your energy with natural vibrations.

SOOTHING NATURE ENERGY: Wear, meditate, sleep, or hold jade and moss agate during times of stress to help soothe your nerves and reduce the effects of stress on your system.

HEALING SESSIONS AND SPACES

I have met very few psychics or spiritual healers in my time who have not been drawn to crystals to help evoke, amplify, and/or channel healing energy, whether for their healing sessions or for their rooms or offices. Because crystals hold, emit, and refract various frequencies of light, they're both an easy and an attractive way to help create a healing and peaceful atmosphere. Those who do therapeutic energy work, in

Continued on page 166

GROUNDING

I met Stephanie at a vegan café in a popular yoga studio downtown. She had such a bright spirit and beautiful energy, and was brimming with great ideas and potential. I watched her as she flitted from table to table, talking to all the people she knew, running late for her class, forgetting her bag, smiles all the way.

She had booked a session with me, and finally arrived 20 minutes late, flustered and scattered and profusely apologetic, and wearing a Herkimer diamond the size of a walnut around her neck. She felt it was helping to keep her connected to Spirit, but it was actually amplifying and magnifying her frazzled state while keeping her from fully connecting with the real world around her.

She confessed she was there because her life was "a hot mess"; she was almost thirty-five and had no real career prospects, no relationship, was just barely making ends meet, and she was sharing an apartment with her ex. She loved to cook vegan food and had come up with the idea of starting a vegan catering company, but was afraid to pursue that venture because she never felt capable of following through on anything. People who had believed in her and supported her in the past didn't take her seriously now because she was "flaky," so she felt hopeless.

The first thing I asked her was "How grounded do you feel? Meaning, how anchored and solid and present in your body do you feel?" Her answer was "Not at all." And that was the problem.

When we're not grounded in our bodies, there's typically not enough energy flowing through our root chakras, so things like managing day-to-day tasks effectively, providing sufficiently for ourselves, feeling energized and healthy, and seeing things through to completion become very challenging. When you're not grounded, it becomes difficult to make positive changes and move forward, because it's the equivalent of spinning your wheels—you can have great ideas, but if you can't ground them in reality, you can't make them happen. It's like not planting a seed but still expecting it to grow.

Staying grounded is also essential to our health and well-being, because it keeps us connected to our vital energy and the vital energy of the Earth, which supports our physical health and our ability to take care of ourselves; fortifies our aura against malevolent entities and psychic attack; keeps us feeling empowered, confident, and capable; and allows for us to be present to and aware of what's going on around us.

Stephanie had prized being spiritual and working with high, spiritual vibrations because she felt this would help her evolve and be a better person. But when she also understood the importance of being grounded, and began to work toward that consistently by wearing crystals like smoky quartz, hematite, and ruby, she slowly started to notice positive changes occurring in her life. Now she's far less forgetful, more prompt, and has secured a solid part-time job to help support herself while she builds a business baking and supplying vegan treats to various yoga studios and cafés in the city. She's still living with her ex and she still wears her Herkimer

GROUNDING

diamond, but for the first time in a long time she feels empowered and capable, and is convinced that a good life is possible for her.

The following is a list of symptoms you may be experiencing or areas of imbalance when you're not fully grounded, and how to address them with crystals.

CRYSTAL COMBINATIONS

EMPOWERMENT AND CONFIDENCE: Wear ruby, bloodstone, and carnelian when needed, or make a crystal tonic to take regularly.

FEELING SCATTERED OR SPACED-OUT: Hold, wear, or meditate with hematite and onyx as needed.

FOLLOW-THROUGH: Wear bloodstone, ruby, onyx, and red jasper daily.

GENERAL GROUNDING: Hold or wear hematite, smoky quartz, bloodstone, red jasper, ruby, shiva lingam, onyx, or jet until you feel grounded. Wear at least one grounding stone daily for maintenance.

LOW ENERGY: Hold or wear ruby, shiva lingam, red jasper, hematite, and infinite daily, or as needed. You can also make a crystal tonic of this combination to take regularly.

LOW SEX DRIVE: Wear or meditate daily with carnelian and shiva lingam, or as needed. Avoid blue tiger eye, as this crystal diminishes sex drive.

MAKING ENDS MEET: Wear or meditate daily with red calcite and ruby.

POOR HEALTH: Wear or sleep with red calcite, bloodstone, hematite, and red jasper daily, or as needed.

PUNCTUALITY: Wear ruby, blue kyanite, and onyx daily.

VULNERABILITY (EMOTIONAL AND PSYCHIC): Wear or sleep with smoky quartz, hematite, and red calcite as needed.

Continued from page 161

particular, can benefit from wearing crystals to increase and sustain the amount of energy they're channeling for a healing session. For a long time I had a large specimen of apophyllite under the middle of my reiki table, which helps to amplify reiki energy, as well as an amethyst cathedral (a large amethyst geode) to radiate soothing, serene energy in my healing room. Many clients would come in, sit down, and remark that as soon as they entered the space they had started to feel better. That's the magic of crystals!

CRYSTAL COMBINATIONS

AMPLIFYING HEALING VIBRATIONS: Wear apophyllite or place a large specimen somewhere central in your healing room or under your therapy table. You can also wear one or two of any of the following crystals: danburite, elestial quartz, ajoite, scolecite, selenite, sugilite, rose quartz, healer's gold, or clear quartz.

CARDS AND DIVINATION TOOLS: Keep a piece of clear quartz and selenite with your card decks and divination tools to absorb lower vibrations and keep your tools' energy strong and clear.

CREATING A SERENE, SOOTHING ATMOSPHERE: Place an amethyst cathedral or geode in front of a window or opposite an open door for serenity and protection, selenite chunks or towers in all corners to purify any stagnating energy, and a clear quartz pyramid in the center of the room to ground healing light. Place a large piece of celestite close to where you and/or your client sits. Place any other crystals you feel drawn to where it feels appropriate.

PAST-LIFE REGRESSION: Tape nuummite, labradorite, and azurite on the underside of the head of the massage table or on the backside of the head of your client's chair, to help facilitate past-life recall or regression, and to help your clients experience their memories and visions more clearly.

PREPARING YOUR VESSEL: Clear your aura by passing a selenite stick down all four sides of your body, above your head and under your feet, and then meditate for 5–30 minutes with rose quartz in your receptive hand and smoky quartz in your dominant hand to feel grounded and heart-centered, and to become a clear, open vessel to receive divine light, energy, and guidance.

THERAPY TABLES: Tape a piece of moldavite, rubellite, and healer's gold on the underside of massage, reiki, or therapeutic tables or chairs to activate and increase healing energies.

MANIFESTATION

The Law of Attraction is perfect and is in operation all the time. We are constantly co-creating our reality with the Universe, whether we're conscious of it or not. The art of manifestation is consciously co-creating our reality, according to our true desires, through our choices, attention, intentions, and energy. I love doing manifestation work with crystals because they make it so much easier and faster, and they can also help clear what's blocking us from achieving our true desires.

I make a point of saying "true desires" because oftentimes where we go wrong with manifestation is when we're trying to co-create something that deep down inside we either don't want or don't believe we can have. We need to be in alignment with what we want, and also be open and willing to receive it, in order for it to come into our experience. Sometimes we may need to work for it; other times it might literally show up on our doorstep. But if we're in alignment with what we truly desire, willing to believe and receive, and working with the right crystals, we can expect results.

If you find when doing this work that you're getting a lot of what you don't want, or didn't think you asked for, take a good look at what's running through your subconscious. Sometimes you might have limiting or negative beliefs, and commitments you've made to those beliefs, that may be gumming up your works. If you suspect that might be the case, do some shadow self work as outlined in Chapter 7, or work with a therapist or life coach to shift those commitments and beliefs.

A final note on manifestation: Make sure that you're clear on what you want. It doesn't need to be defined down to the very last detail, as that could start to limit the options the Universe has to send to you, but if you're vague and wishy-washy, you'll get vague and wishy-washy results. Be empowered, clear, and excited about what you want! Remember: This is energy work, and energy moves according to your direction, regardless of whether you're a thief or a saint. When you understand that energy is neutral, and it's all in how you use it, then you have much more power to decide if you want to be creating positive or negative experiences in your life.

Work with your manifestation crystals daily until you have achieved the results you desire.

CRYSTAL COMBINATIONS

ACTION: Wear or hold pyrite while taking action toward whatever you're seeking to manifest. As an alternative, you can lie down and spend 10–30 minutes with it placed on your solar plexus chakra daily while visualizing your goal.

ALIGNMENT AND CLARITY: If you need more clarity, or if you want assurance that what you're seeking to manifest is in alignment with your true desires, meditate on it or journal while holding eudialyte and sodalite. These crystals support us in finding ourselves in moments of silence, and hearing our heart's desires in those moments, so that we can then pursue them faithfully.

BELIEVING: If your outlook, mood, or expectation is limited or negative, then the circumstances or results you manifest will be, too. Meditate with chrysanthemum stone to shift your expectations, outlook, and thus fortunes in your favor.

MEDITATION: Hold a quartz point and clear topaz in your receptive hand, and another quartz point and epidote in your dominant hand, while spending 5–15 minutes meditating on whatever you're seeking to attract or manifest.

RECEIVING: If you feel unworthy of what you're seeking to manifest, wear green aventurine, sugilite, and watermelon tourmaline; sleep with them at night; or make a crystal tonic and take it five times daily.

SURRENDER: There often comes a point in manifestation work where you feel guided to leave it in the hands of the Divine, to trust the process, flow, and timing of the Universe. This can be challenging, especially if the need to control interferes. Holding or meditating with angelite when that fear or resistance arises, or sleeping with it nightly, helps us relax, be still, and have faith in the Higher Forces at work.

VISUALIZATION: Hold optical calcite or lie down and place it on your third eye chakra, while visualizing whatever you're seeking to attract, experience, or create.

VOCALIZATION: I once heard a big Broadway star emphasize that if you wanted something, you had to say it out loud; that giving it voice gave it power. Wear or hold blue apatite while speaking out your desires or intentions to help increase this power.

MEDITATION

Holding crystals while meditating is one of my favorite ways of working with crystals, but crystals also help you meditate. Starting a meditation practice may be challenging and frustrating, and there are times in our practice when a little added help is appreciated. Holding crystals while meditating can help improve and support your practice.

CRYSTAL COMBINATIONS

ANXIETY: If you start to experience anxiety while meditating, or feel too anxious to meditate, hold lithium quartz or angelite in your receptive hand and smoky quartz in your dominant hand to soothe your nerves and clear some of the anxious energy from your system.

CONNECTION: If you want to feel more open and connected to Source and All-That-Is, hold selenite in your receptive hand to help expand your crown chakra and fill you with a sense of serenity and peace.

DROWSINESS: If you meditate when you first wake up, or find that you're having trouble staying awake while meditating, hold a shiva lingam in each hand to help you feel more energized, present, and centered.

QUIET MIND: If you find that you're suffering from "monkey mind"—that is, thoughts just keep whirling around inside your head—hold blue lace agate in your receptive hand and smoky quartz in your dominant hand to help calm, ground, and gather your thoughts into stillness.

PROTECTION

Energy protection is a way of sealing in your aura and keeping your energy safe within a positive, high vibration of energy or light frequencies. It's a way to keep you from being adversely affected or influenced by lower, harmful energy from other people, places, things, intentions, curses, entities, or thought-forms. It's particularly valuable for those who are empathic and/or sensitive to energy, but it's good to keep in practice even for those who are not, as we are all ultimately beings of light and energy and can therefore be adversely affected whether we are aware of it or not. I never leave my home without wearing at least one protective crystal, and the most common question I am asked is this: "Which crystals are good for protection?"

Protective crystals need to be worn and cleared daily, and in some cases, depending on the energy you're dealing with, they may need to be cleared several times a day. If you're troubled at night when you sleep, or if you're concerned that someone may be directing malevolent energy your way, it's also best to sleep with protective crystals under your pillow or by your bedside at night. Crystals by your bedside will need to be at least the size of a deck of cards to be effective (roughly 3"/7.5cm in diameter); crystals under your pillow need to be at least 1.5"/.8cm in diameter or larger, depending on which size is comfortable.

CRYSTAL COMBINATIONS

AURA CLOAKING: Fluorite will help make your aura frequency hard to tune into for anyone who is sending curses or malevolent energy your way. It's important that the fluorite contain all four of its natural rays of color (purple, blue, green, and yellow) in order to be effective.

AURA SHIELDING: Black tourmaline will shield your aura from lower or harmful vibrations. Black tourmaline helps raise the energy frequency of your aura. It acts very much like an electrified fence, repelling negative energy.

DREAM SAFETY: Place labradorite, staurolite, and moonstone under your pillow, or in a pouch around your neck, to keep your dreams epic, memorable, and safe while you're on the dream plane. I had a necklace of labradorite and moonstone beads strung for me to wear at night specifically for this purpose.

EMPATHS: Jet will help to absorb a lot of lower, harmful energy and debris in your stead, but will need to be cleared several times a day or it is likely to fall and break.

PSYCHIC SHIELD: Wear labradorite, fluorite, black tourmaline, black obsidian, and blue kyanite to shield yourself from psychic attack, entity attachment, curses, witchcraft, and evil.

SLEEP SAFETY: Place celestite, black obsidian, spirit quartz, black tourmaline, and amethyst either under your pillow or beside your bed to ward off lower, harmful spirits while sleeping. For added protection, place a long selenite stick on the floor on either side of your bed, and hematite under the head and foot of your mattress.

....

STRESS AND CONFLICT REPELLENT: Wear black tourmaline, blue kyanite, smoky quartz, jet, and rose quartz to keep from being affected or influenced by other people's stress, anger, and/or negativity, while still being able to remain grounded, compassionate, and neutral in your responses.

PSYCHIC ABILITIES

Strengthening your intuition and activating or expanding your psychic abilities—what is often referred to as opening your third eye chakra—is the easiest thing to do with crystals. Even if you're working with them for other purposes, heightened intuitive and sixth senses will be a natural side effect. From a young age, I could see things at night, was highly sensitive, and was also a lucid dreamer (meaning that I was conscious that I was dreaming while in the dream state). But it was when I started working with crystals to cultivate my abilities that I saw rapid and substantial improvements in my capabilities.

There are some things to bear in mind when working on your psychic abilities: Some people will be stronger in certain areas than others, but each of us has intuition, and each of us has extrasensory abilities that we can develop. If you try to push the development of your abilities too fast or too hard, you're likely to block yourself and experience limited improvement. The key thing is to honor your process, and also to pay attention. If you're working on developing your intuition, follow your hunches. If you're working on your clairvoyance, pay attention to what you're seeing, especially out of the corners of your eyes. People have a tendency to dismiss what they're experiencing when it's unusual or challenges their conventional beliefs, so remain open and curious when doing this work.

CRYSTAL COMBINATIONS

BLOCKAGE OR BURNOUT: If you feel that you've blocked an ability as a result of pushing it too hard, or if you've been relying on an ability a lot lately and feel burned out, you can work with specific crystals to undo the damage. Placing clear calcite on any relevant chakra for 20–60 minutes will help to clear blockage and restore the chakra. Do this as often as needed, and then resume your development work gently. If you're a professional psychic and need to give your third eye chakra a quick reboot, I've found that azurite is extremely effective.

CLAIRAUDIENCE: The ability to hear spirits, energy, and guidance is located primarily in the throat chakra, though some believe that it's also located in either the third eye chakra or in ear chakras near the temples. People who are clairaudient typically have more sensitive hearing, and loud or piercing noises have a tendency to cause them great discomfort. At the same time, they are almost always music lovers. Wear or meditate holding azurite, celestite, angelite, chrysocolla, blue kyanite, or aqua aura quartz in your receptive hand to activate and strengthen this ability. You can also lie down and place one or two of these stones on your throat chakra for 30–60 minutes a week. Just make sure that they're small, so that they don't create any physical discomfort. You can also make a crystal tonic from one or more of these stones and take it regularly for a slower, more gradual process.

CLAIRCOGNIZANCE: The ability to receive guidance, knowledge, prophecy, information, and details in the form of thoughts, memories, or words in your mind is located in the crown chakra. People who are claircognizant have a tendency toward greater intelligence, are ambidextrous, and are usually able to learn, process, and memorize information more quickly than others. Meditate holding selenite, scolecite, sugilite, danburite, amethyst, elestial quartz, labradorite, nuummite, moldavite, apophyllite, blue kyanite, or hiddenite in your receptive hand to activate and strengthen this ability. You can also lie down and place two or three of these stones at the top of your head for 30–60 minutes a week. If you wish to wear a crystal for daily development, avoid selenite, danburite, or scolecite, as they can space you out and leave you feeling very ungrounded, potentially making you vulnerable to accidents, hazards, and psychic attack.

CLAIRSENTIENCE: The ability to feel or sense the presence of spirits, energy, emotions, and guidance is located primarily in the solar plexus chakra. Wear or meditate holding tiger eye, honey calcite, citrine, chrysocolla, pietersite, sugilite, infinite, staurolite, or chiastolite in your receptive hand to activate and strengthen this ability. You can also lie down and place two or three of these stones on your solar plexus chakra for 30–60 minutes a week. I have found, too, that making a crystal tonic with a few of these stones has been highly effective for the development of this ability.

CLAIRVOYANCE: The ability to see spirits, energy, and through the veils of time, space, and reality is located primarily in your third eye chakra. Clairvoyants tend to be visual learners and thinkers, vivid dreamers, sensitive to bright or flashing lights, and exceedingly creative. Wear or meditate holding chiastolite, azurite, moldavite, sugilite, Herkimer diamond, amethyst, fluorite, optical calcite, or lepidolite in your receptive hand to activate and strengthen this ability. You can also lie down and place two or three of these crystals on your third eye chakra for 60 minutes once or twice a week.

DIVINATION: Wear amethyst, Herkimer diamond, sugilite, azurite, and ajoite when doing any kind of divinatory work for increased accuracy, clarity, and receptivity to guidance. If you are doing psychic readings for other people, replace the Herkimer diamond with jet so you have an added amount of psychic protection, and so you're less likely to take on any of your clients' energy. As an alternative, you can wear moldavite and sugilite, or meditate with that combination before engaging in your work. Always be sure to remove and clear your crystals when you're finished.

DREAMWORK: To have more vivid dreams, or to experience lucid or prophetic dreams, sleep with moonstone, Herkimer diamond, lepidolite, scolecite, and labradorite under your pillow. You can also make a crystal tonic using this combination and take it regularly before bed. The lepidolite's main function is to balance out the energizing effect of the Herkimer diamond, but if you find you're having trouble sleeping, replace the Herkimer diamond with selenite. To help facilitate dream recall the next day, hold a Herkimer diamond in your receptive hand while journaling. An alternative to placing crystals under your pillow is to meditate holding moonstone in your receptive hand and labradorite in your dominant hand for 10–20 minutes before napping or going to bed.

FEAR: People often block their natural abilities because they're afraid of what they might see, hear, or experience. Meditate regularly, holding sugilite and amethyst, to start working through this fear. Additionally, you can hold these two crystals while lying down with clear calcite on your third eye chakra, and rubellite and rhodochrosite on your heart chakra for 60 minutes once or twice a week. To discover the root cause of a fear-based block, meditate with labradorite or hold it in your receptive hand while writing down your stream of consciousness.

INTUITION: The key to working with crystals for intuition is consistency—the more often you work with them, the more quickly your intuition will develop. Wear or meditate with any two of the following on a regular basis: amethyst, shiva lingam, azurite, danburite, Herkimer diamond, staurolite, citrine, moldavite, sugilite, chiastolite, pietersite, blue tiger eye, moonstone, ajoite, or tiger eye. If you find that you're having trouble trusting and following your intuition, wear or meditate daily with shiva lingam, pietersite, and blue tiger eye. Pay closer attention to your feelings, instincts, and thoughts, and make a note of things that repeatedly draw your attention or attract your eye. Every human being has intuition, and there is no limit to how accurate and powerful yours can become, provided you're willing to trust and honor it. It's been my experience, as well as that of my clients, that the more you follow it, the better off you'll be.

OPENING YOUR THIRD EYE CHAKRA: Lie down with sugilite, amethyst, azurite, and Herkimer diamond on your third eye chakra for 60 minutes. (As an alternative, you can use one piece of moldavite.) One time should suffice, but you can repeat this if you feel it's necessary, or if you want to give your intuition a mega-boost. This is a combination that can be overpowering, so trust how you're feeling; if it feels like too much, remove the crystals immediately and follow one of the intuition-boosting protocols instead.

part **3**

DO-IT-YOURSELF CRYSTAL HEALING

Crystal Healing Layouts

WHAT'S A CRYSTAL HEALING LAYOUT? Simply put, it's a specific placement of crystals on the body to effect healing. This is what many crystal healers do (though not all) when you go to see one professionally for a healing session. The beauty of this work is that you can do it by yourself, in the comfort of your own home, and for free once you've bought your crystals. The layouts I'll be sharing with you are based on the Hindu seven-chakra system, so we need to have a crash course on that first.

THE CHAKRA SYSTEM

The word *chakra* comes from Sanskrit, meaning "spinning wheel of light." Chakras are major energy centers, coinciding with major nerve centers in the body. They spiral outward into the four subtle bodies of the aura (the physical, mental, emotional, and spiritual layers of the aura).

When a chakra is not functioning properly, it can trigger physical, mental, emotional, or spiritual health issues. There are hundreds of chakras in our body, but this system is based on the seven main chakras: the root, sacral, solar plexus, heart, throat, third eye, and crown. There are many different philosophies and systems based on the chakras, but in crystal healing I have found working with these seven to be the most effective.

ROOT CHAKRA

The root chakra is red and is located at the base of the spine. It is the foundation of the physical body. It stimulates physical activity, exercise, action, and vitality; assists us in keeping grounded and present; and influences our immune system, basic instincts, endurance, and fight-or-flight reactions. This chakra manages the body's survival needs, including food, shelter, and protection. Family and tribal (i.e., societal and cultural) relationships influence the well-being of this chakra. It is relevant to achievements in the material world, permanence, strength of character, patience, endurance, and safety.

If you're having trouble making ends meet; always feel spaced-out, tired, and sick; have fear or control issues; or experienced childhood trauma, you may have an imbalance in the root chakra.

In general, crystals that are black, gray, brown, and red resonate with the root chakra.

SACRAL CHAKRA

The sacral chakra is orange and is located below the belly button. The sacral chakra is the foundation of the emotional body and is the source of creativity, emotions, and pleasure. It governs our ability to feel and manage our emotions and experience sensations. The sacral chakra influences our sexuality and sensuality, intimacy, and ability to be social with other people. It physically influences the lower abdomen, bladder, kidneys, digestion, reproduction, and virility.

If you find that you are often moody, seek to be alone, or are overly needy of other people; if you have eating, drug, alcohol, or sexual issues; or if you're having trouble conceiving a child, you may have a sacral chakra imbalance.

In general, crystals that are red, orange, and yellow resonate with the sacral chakra.

SOLAR PLEXUS CHAKRA

The solar plexus chakra is yellow and is located just below the rib cage. It is the foundation of the mental body. It enables us to sense vibrations and essences from people, places, and things. It's our personal power center, where our sense of identity and confidence, our will, our ambition, our ability to manifest and prosper, and our personal drive are located. It physically influences muscles, the stomach, digestion, the pancreas, the liver, the gallbladder, metabolism, the immune system, the kidneys, and the nervous system.

If you feel apathetic, unable to improve your life or prosper; if you're prone to angry outbursts, are easily dominated, or have ulcers or digestive issues, you may have a solar plexus chakra imbalance.

In general, crystals that are orange, yellow, or gold resonate with the solar plexus chakra.

HEART CHAKRA

The heart chakra is green and is situated in the center of the chest, just slightly above the heart. While the lower three chakras relate to personal energy and the physical self, and the higher three chakras relate to the spiritual self, the heart chakra bridges the two and forms a connection between our physical and our spiritual experiences. It is all about love—experiencing it, feeling it, sharing it—and it governs forgiveness, compassion, empathy, trust, and equilibrium. The heart chakra helps us to get in touch with nature and connects us to the plant and animal world. This chakra physically influences the lungs, the thymus, circulation, and the endocrine and immune systems.

If you've experienced a lot of heartbreak; if you're mourning, have intimacy issues, are frequently sick with respiratory or heart-related illnesses; or if you are depressed, you may have a heart chakra imbalance.

In general, crystals that are pink, red, and green resonate with the heart chakra.

THROAT CHAKRA

Situated in the center of the throat, the throat chakra is light blue and influences communication, artistic expression, authenticity, self-awareness, honesty, and clairaudience (the psychic ability of hearing spirits). Physically, it influences the mouth, the teeth, the throat, the thyroid gland, and the immune system. When it is balanced, it allows for free communication, an ease in articulating ideas, and a grounded, present ability and willingness to listen, both to ourselves and to others. We are able to lovingly honor our boundaries when the throat chakra is in balance. It also helps us while we are meditating to connect with our higher guidance.

If you're afraid to speak up for yourself, you repress your feelings, you block your creative impulses, you ignore your intuition, or you experience frequent throat illnesses, you may have a throat chakra imbalance.

In general, blue-green and light blue crystals resonate with the throat chakra.

THIRD EYE CHAKRA

The third eye chakra is indigo and is found in the middle of the forehead. It is the foundation of our psychic and cognitive (thinking) abilities. It enables us to listen to and honor our intuition and imagination; to learn, visualize, focus, and remember; and it also helps us determine the difference between fantasy and reality. This chakra physically influences the eyes, vision, the nose, the central nervous system, the brain, the pineal gland, and the pituitary gland.

If you frequently experience brain fog, feel that your intuition is blocked, have trouble remembering things, or struggle with anxiety or a mental disorder, you may have a third eye chakra imbalance.

In general, crystals that are clear, dark blue, or purple resonate with the third eye chakra.

CROWN CHAKRA

The crown chakra is violet and is situated on the top of the head. It is the foundation of our spiritual body and links us to higher guidance, our own wisdom, memory, spirituality, and the Divine. It influences our ability to have faith, our religious or spiritual beliefs, our philosophy, our perspective, our idealism, and our archetypal knowledge. It is our connection with the Universe/God/Goddess/Spirit. This chakra physically influences the cerebral cortex, the cerebrum, the central nervous system, the pineal gland, the pituitary gland, and hormones related to them.

If you have trouble making up your mind, are easily led or influenced by other people or belief systems, ignore your own spiritual needs, have memory problems, or have lost faith, you may have a crown chakra imbalance.

In general, white, clear, lavender, or gold crystals resonate with the crown chakra.

BEGINNER'S LAYOUT

With crystal layouts, it's always best to start out small and easy, and test out how they feel or affect you before moving on to bigger crystals or more involved work. Why? So you can familiarize yourself with crystal energy and you can have a benchmark to compare the effects and feelings of certain crystals when working with them. I have seen some intensely elaborate and terrifying crystal layouts in books and at workshops. It's been my experience that keeping it simple and straightforward is usually best.

Practicing crystal layouts on myself was actually how I got started in crystal healing and the only real training I've ever had. Day after day, even if I only had 5 or 10 minutes, I'd lay some crystals out on my seven chakras, lie back and relax, and let the energy flow. After that I'd make notes of what I used, how I felt, and the progress I was witnessing in certain areas of my life.

The truth was, too, that I needed a lot of healing and help at that time. I was still building back up from an emotional and financial rock bottom; I was still in a lot of pain, racked with doubt and anger; and I didn't have the money to see a therapist or work much with a spiritual healer. My crystals became my salvation, my teachers, my healers, a place where I could always go and receive healing energy. Not only did they get me through that hard time, but I progressed exponentially as a healer, a spiritualist, a mystic, and a businessperson as a result of my work with them.

My third eye opened, my heart softened, I learned and absorbed new information rapidly, my intuitive guidance became clearer, my ability to channel energy became stronger, and my tiny little healing practice began to grow and grow. I was far from healed and I was not yet prospering, but in a few short months, I was light-years away from where I had been before.

The first layout I ever started working with is still a favorite of mine to this day. I call it a beginner's, or basic, layout. I still use this one when I need a restorative energy session. It helps to clear out stagnant energy, restore balance, and increase vitality and overall sense of well-being. It's great at the end of a long, stressful day or week, and it's the foundation layout on which the rest of the layouts in this section are based. (See Beginner's Layout diagram and chart on pages 194 and 195.)

LAYOUTS

On the following pages you will find a variety of different crystal layouts. Make sure that your crystals have been cleared and that they're charged before doing a layout. I find it easiest to put my crystals on a tray and then place the tray beside me where I'm lying down so that I can access them easily without having to sit up. Always place crystals in ascending order (starting with the root chakra and working your way up) and then remove them in descending order (from the crown chakra down) in order to remain grounded.

Depending on the layout, some chakras will require the placement of more than one crystal. As a general rule of thumb, you can always go slightly larger in size with crystals on the root, sacral, solar plexus, and heart chakras because their energy is more dense and physical in nature. The three upper chakras (throat, third eye, and crown) are more sensitive and need less crystal energy for positive effects. On a practical note, you have less surface space to work with when you're placing crystals on the

Continued on page 196

BEGINNER'S LAYOUT

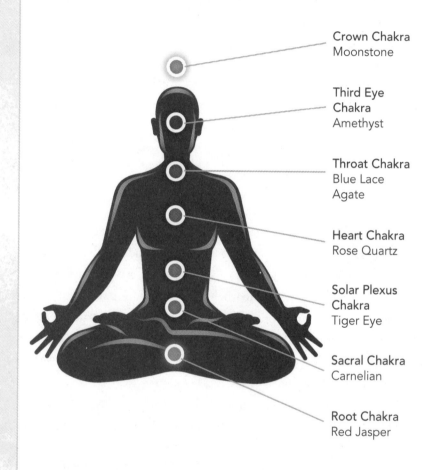

Crown Chakra
Moonstone

Third Eye Chakra
Amethyst

Throat Chakra
Blue Lace Agate

Heart Chakra
Rose Quartz

Solar Plexus Chakra
Tiger Eye

Sacral Chakra
Carnelian

Root Chakra
Red Jasper

CHAKRA	CRYSTAL
Root Chakra	Red Jasper
Sacral Chakra	Carnelian
Solar Plexus Chakra	Tiger Eye
Heart Chakra	Rose Quartz
Throat Chakra	Blue Lace Agate
Third Eye Chakra	Amethyst
Crown Chakra	Moonstone

three upper chakras. I also recommend having a blanket nearby in case you get cold during your session, and a timer close at hand.

Crystal therapy sessions normally run anywhere from 20 to 60 minutes. I don't recommend going longer than an hour because there's only so much energy your body can take in a single session. If you make the session too short, you won't benefit as much from the layout. After your session, drink plenty of water and you can eat something light or go for a leisurely walk, but avoid vigorous activity, alcoholic consumption, or high sugar intake for at least one hour after your session.

Enjoy!

HEALTH AND VITALITY	FERTILITY	IMMUNE BOOSTING
Root—red calcite, ruby, red jasper	Root—ruby, red calcite	Root—ruby, red calcite, red jasper
Sacral—orange calcite, carnelian	Sacral—carnelian, shiva lingam, garnet	Sacral—bloodstone, orange calcite
Solar plexus—citrine	Solar plexus—citrine	Solar plexus—citrine, honey calcite
Heart—green aventurine	Heart—mangano calcite, rose quartz	Heart—green calcite, green aventurine
Throat—blue calcite	Throat—blue lace agate	Throat—aquamarine
Third eye—azurite	Third eye—sugilite	Third eye—fluorite
Crown—clear calcite	Crown—moonstone	Crown—celestite

SELF-LOVE	CREATIVITY	STRESS RELIEF
Root—ruby, apache tear	Root—ruby, shiva lingam	Root—smoky quartz, black tourmaline
Sacral—garnet	Sacral—carnelian, orange calcite, garnet	Sacral—orange calcite, bloodstone
Solar plexus—honey calcite, rhodochrosite	Solar plexus—citrine, cinnabar quartz	Solar plexus—honey calcite, tiger eye
Heart—rose quartz, mangano calcite, watermelon tourmaline	Heart—rubellite	Heart—lithium quartz, rose quartz, green calcite
Throat—chrysocolla	Throat—blue kyanite	Throat—blue calcite
Third eye—sodalite	Third eye—azurite	Third eye—amethyst
Crown—moonstone	Crown—moonstone, selenite	Crown—selenite

LUCK (ENERGY SHIFT)	PSYCHIC DEVELOPMENT	PROSPERITY
Root—ruby, chrysanthemum stone	Root—elestial quartz, snowflake obsidian	Root—ruby, chrysanthemum stone
Sacral—bloodstone	Sacral—shiva lingam	Sacral—bloodstone, garnet
Solar plexus—citrine, cinnabar quartz	Solar plexus—tiger eye	Solar plexus—pyrite, citrine
Heart—hiddenite, jade, green aventurine	Heart—watermelon tourmaline, rubellite	Heart—emerald, jade, eudialyte
Throat—blue lace agate	Throat—celestite	Throat—blue apatite
Third eye—amethyst	Third eye—azurite, sugilite	Third eye—azurite, blue sapphire
Crown—clear calcite	Crown—moonstone, ajoite	Crown—clear calcite, moonstone

CHAPTER

10

Crystal Healing Baths

READ THAT THERE'S A CELEBRITY SPA IN BRAZIL that has a pool lined with forty thousand pieces of green quartz, charging the water with its healing, rejuvenating properties. But you don't need to travel to Brazil to experience some of this magic—you can do it for yourself in your own bathtub! The benefit of a crystal bath is that your system absorbs larger amounts of crystal energy in shorter periods of time, accelerating healing, boosting your mood or energy, calming or soothing your mind, bolstering your psychic defenses, and altering or enhancing your vibration to attract whatever you want, quickly and easily.

I fell in love with taking crystal baths because it was such a powerful and effective way of receiving crystal healing while in a state of total relaxation. Crystal baths became a regular habit of mine to help clear, heal, and restore my energy, and I regularly recommend them to both my clients and my students. You get a lot of bang for your buck here because, along with the energy healing component, the added combination of salt helps to physically cleanse and draw toxins out of the body, and the herbs or oils are good for the skin. Win-win-win!

Most important is for you to stick to the combinations I suggest or thoroughly research the geological and mineral properties of alternate crystals before putting them in your water. Some crystals and stones can be highly toxic (like cinnabar, which is composed of mercury sulfide, or malachite, which is composed of hydrous copper carbonate). Only use polished or tumbled stones, and, if in doubt, go without.

Based on my research and experience, I have not found any of the crystals in this chapter to be harmful or to have any adverse effects when bathing with them, but it's always best to use caution. You can make a large batch of crystal tonic using the safe method described in this book and add that to your bathwater as a 100 percent safe alternative. Also, bear in mind that some people's skin may be more sensitive than others', so if your skin tends to be sensitive, you may want to skip the addition of flower petals, salts, or essential oils suggested in the bath protocols here. Do a patch test first to check for any potential allergic reactions.

In terms of size, you'll want to work with crystals that are at least the size of a deck of cards or larger to alter the vibration of your bathwater. The bigger the crystal, the more energy it emits and the greater the effect it has on the energy of the water. If you can't find big pieces, you can group together several smaller pieces to make up for the size. Imagine soaking in a tub full of crystal energy! That's what we're creating here.

Make sure you've cleared your crystals first and that you've also cleaned them with soap or wiped them down with rubbing alcohol. Your bathtub needs to be clean and if you're using any oils, make sure they are therapeutic-grade essential oils or holistic herbal oils. If you're using flower petals, make sure they haven't been sprayed with pesticides. Sea salt and herbs from your local grocery store are fine. Sea salt or Epsom salt can substitute for any of the other suggested salts, if need be.

Drink a full glass of water before taking your bath. Placing crystals in salted water for these purposes is likely to deplete their energy, so they will need to be charged after your bath. Rinsing off quickly in a shower afterwards will help to clear the salt off your hair and skin. If you want to multitask your bath with your regular cleansing and grooming routine, you can, but it's nice to keep this time exclusively for energy work.

The crystals need to stand in the bathwater for a full 20 minutes before it's ready for you to soak in, so make the water a little warmer than you would normally and test the temperature before climbing in. You can also remove the crystals first, but make sure to rinse them off in cool running water after you're done.

CRYSTAL COMBINATIONS

ABUNDANCE BATH: Place citrine, bloodstone, and jade in your tub. Fill with water and toss in 2 cups/473ml of sea salt. Allow the water to stand for 20 minutes. Remove crystals and rinse them under cool, clear water, and then soak in your tub for 20 minutes. Visualize wealth and/or material possessions coming to you while you're in the bath.

....

AURA-CLEARING BATH: Our auras are the natural protective layer of energy that surrounds us and protects us from negative or harmful psychic energy. When our auras are filled or covered with negative debris (stress, fear, spiteful intentions, other people's energy, and the like) they may become weakened and damaged, rendering them less effective and also possibly compromising our health. By clearing our auric fields on a regular basis, we keep them strong and healthy. Place amethyst, black obsidian, and clear quartz in your tub. Fill with water and toss in 2 cups/473ml of Dead Sea salt or sea salt. It's important to fully submerge yourself in the water at least seven times so that you are cleared from head to toe.

....

CALM HEART, QUIET MIND BATH: Place blue lace agate, smoky quartz, and blue calcite in your tub. Fill with water and toss in 2 cups/473ml of sea salt. Juicy addition: Light some vanilla or floral-scented candles, play soft classical music, and pour a few drops of lavender, vanilla, or myrrh oil in the water.

....

DETOX BATH: Place red calcite, smoky quartz, and green calcite in your tub. Fill with water and toss in 1 cup/237ml of sea salt and

1 cup/237ml of natural baking soda. Juicy addition: Add a few drops of lavender or cedarwood oil for a soothing, restorative effect; you can also put in ¼ cup/59ml of bentonite clay for an added detox effect.

HEALING BATH: Place green, orange, and red calcite, and citrine in your tub. Fill with water and toss in 2 cups/473ml of Himalayan salt.

LOVE-INVITING BATH: Place rose quartz, pink opal, and jade in your tub. Fill with water and toss in 1 cup/237ml of plain sea salt and 1 cup/237ml of pink Himalayan salt. Juicy addition: Light rose-scented candles, scatter a handful of red rose petals onto the water, and play soft, romantic, classical music.

MOOD AND ENERGY-BOOSTING BATH: Place citrine, bloodstone, and red jasper in your tub. Fill with water and toss in 2 cups/473ml of Dead Sea, Celtic, or Epsom salt. Juicy addition: Pour a few drops of citrus, cedar, rosemary, or mint essential oil.

SELF-WORTH AND CONFIDENCE-BOOSTING BATH: Place rose quartz, citrine, and amethyst in your tub. Fill with water and toss in 1 cup/237ml of pink Himalayan salt and 1 cup of sea salt. Juicy addition: Pour a few drops of citrus or frankincense oil into your bath.

SPIRIT BATH: To invite prophetic dreams or enhance your psychic abilities, place clear calcite, amethyst, and quartz in your tub. Fill with water and toss in 1 cup/237ml Himalayan salt and 1 cup Dead Sea salt. Juicy addition: Place your hands, palms facing down, over the surface of the water, say a prayer, and bless the water before getting in.

CHAPTER

11

Crystal Tonics

STARTED MAKING CRYSTAL TONICS to help provide daily crystal support for clients who were in the fashion and film industries and couldn't wear crystals while they were working. These also worked out well for clients who traveled often and needed to travel light. The art of making crystal tonics involves infusing spring water with crystal energy and then preserving it either with a distilled spirit (preferably brandy or vodka) or with vinegar (apple cider vinegar works best). It's a fairly simple method; it just takes a little time and requires some supplies. The key thing to working with tonics is that they need to be taken regularly and consistently in order to work, as they have a cumulative effect. The effects are subtle at first but over time (anywhere from 2 to 4 weeks) you should really be able to notice the difference.

SUPPLIES

- 16 ounces/473ml spring water

- Crystal combination (crystals should be anywhere from 1"–3"/2.5cm–7.5cm in size)

- Glass pitcher

- Glass test tube or slender glass container that fits inside the glass pitcher (for method #1)

- Glass jar with tight-fitting lid

- 3–5 single-terminated quartz points, anywhere from 1"–2"/2.5cm–5cm long (for method #2)

- Plastic wrap or cheesecloth

- 1 ounce/30ml glass bottle with dropper

- Adhesive label or masking tape and a marker

- 8 ounces/237ml vodka, brandy, or apple cider vinegar

STEPS FOR MAKING A CRYSTAL TONIC (METHOD #1)

1. Clear the energy of your crystals (see page 23).

2. Clean your glass pitcher, test tube or inner glass container, jar with lid, and bottle. I find it best to either run them through a sanitizing wash in your dishwasher, or to sanitize your test tube or inner glass container by placing them in a large pot of boiling water for a few minutes.

3. Fill the glass pitcher with spring water.

4. Place your crystal combination in the test tube, and the test tube in the glass pitcher. Be certain that your crystals do not come in direct contact with the water.

5. Cover the top of the pitcher with either plastic wrap or cheesecloth to keep the water free of debris.

6. Let stand for 3–7 days undisturbed.

7. Remove the test tube, pour the infused water from the pitcher into the jar, and then blend with the vodka, brandy, or vinegar.

8. Add a small amount of the mixture to your bottle with a dropper, and keep the rest as your mother stock to refill when needed. Label both with type, ingredients, and date, and keep your mother stock in a dark, cool dry place. It should keep for up to six months.

STEPS FOR MAKING A CRYSTAL TONIC (METHOD #2)

1. Clear the energy of your crystals (see page 23).

2. Clean your glass pitcher.

3. Fill the glass pitcher with spring water.

4. Place the same number of single-terminated quartz crystals as in your crystal combination around the pitcher, pointing in toward the pitcher.

5. Place each one of your crystals from your combination at the flat end of your quartz points, so that the point is directing the crystal's energy toward the water in the pitcher.

6. Cover the top of the pitcher with either plastic wrap or cheesecloth to keep the water free of debris.

7. Let stand for 7 days undisturbed.

8. Remove crystals, pour the infused water from the pitcher into the jar, and then blend with the vodka, brandy, or vinegar.

9. Add a small amount of the mixture to your bottle with a dropper, and keep the rest as your mother stock to refill when needed. Label both with type, ingredients, and date, and keep your mother stock in a cool, dark, dry place.

CRYSTAL TONIC RECIPES

The following tonics are from my own little recipe book. I made these over and over again and my clients experienced successful results. However, if you want to switch things up or make additions, by all means go ahead! Just please stick to the safe method and never place crystals directly in your drinking water because many of them can be toxic.

ADRENAL RESTORATIVE: ocean jasper, chrysocolla, shiva lingam, citrine.

CALM: blue lace agate, lithium quartz, smoky quartz, amethyst.

COURAGE: ruby, red jasper, aquamarine, amazonite, rhodonite.

DIGESTIVE TONIC (FOR INFLAMMATORY CONDITIONS): celestite, aquamarine, bloodstone, tiger eye.

DIGESTIVE TONIC (FOR SLUGGISH CONDITIONS): fire agate, pyrite, citrine, honey calcite, orange calcite.

EMPOWERMENT: ruby, garnet, carnelian, red jasper, amazonite.

ENERGY: red jasper, rutilated quartz (gold or copper colored rutile), pyrite, infinite.

GROUNDING: red jasper, ruby, hematite, jet, bloodstone.

HEART HEALING (EMOTIONAL): malachite, mangano calcite, rose quartz, rhodochrosite.

IMMUNE BOOSTER: red jasper, honey calcite, citrine, green aventurine, green calcite.

LOVE: rose quartz, rhodonite, rhodochrosite, ruby, garnet.

PSYCHIC ABILITY: amethyst, chiastolite, moonstone, sugilite, azurite.

PSYCHIC PROTECTION: amethyst, black tourmaline, staurolite, fluorite, black obsidian.

STRESS RELIEF: smoky quartz, selenite, rose quartz, amethyst, blue calcite.

TRANSFORMATION: three pieces of moldavite, one amethyst, one moonstone.

You deserve to feel good about yourself, be healthy, and know that you're worthy of so many great things. It's up to you to open up and allow this for yourself, and I hope that this book and your crystal allies will be of benefit to you on your healing journey. Whether it's shifting your mind-set, trying something new, going for it, finding ways to enjoy life more, or investing in your abilities, always say yes to yourself! When you say yes to yourself, you're saying yes to life, and great and wondrous possibilities follow.

Crystal blessings to you all!

Acknowledgments

THIS BOOK IS MY LOVE LETTER to all the crystals in my healing kit, on my shelves, and in my heart, for helping me and countless others heal, grow, and find grace. I am truly, truly blessed to have discovered their healing light.

My most heartfelt gratitude to Susan Lander for her incredible generosity, support, kindness, insight, and guidance, and for holding my hand throughout this process. Thank you to Colleen Duffy for being my spiritual mentor, guide, and teacher.

I am so grateful to my mom for all her unconditional love, incredible patience, support, faith, and copious copy editing, for always putting us kids first and for never giving up on us. I want to send special gratitude to Anjelika Kremer, who first told me that I had a gift; to Rosemary Brocco for introducing me to the healing power of stones; and to C.B.V. for keeping me this side of the border.

I am so very thankful for all the hours my dear friends Nicholas Pepe and Elsa Mehary spent reading sections of this book and providing feedback, suggestions, and encouragement, and for their steadfast and loving support. Special thanks, Nicholas, for blessing this book with your magic and healing energy. Thank you to Erik House and fellow faery Rachael Shaffer for taking time out of their busy schedules to help edit and advise.

Very special thanks to Kate Zimmermann and everyone at Sterling Publishing for giving me the opportunity to publish this book and bring it out into the world. And to all my clients for trusting me with their process, sharing their stories, and allowing me to be a part of their healing journey, I thank you.

Muchas graçias Ingrid Aybar, for your wisdom, insight, and galvanizing advice. I'm sending so much heartfelt gratitude to my beautiful family and friends for always believing in me, supporting me, and being a part of my life: JD, Jeanette, Sonja, Rabeea, Roberto, Nancy, Fianna, Vanessa, and my furry kids Gaby and Muppet.

Love and blessings to all of you,
and to all of those who read this book.

IMAGE CREDITS

AJOITE

High-vibration crystal that connects you to angelic frequencies and higher divine guidance, and fills your system with divine light. Clears the aura of cords and entity attachments. Amplifies psychic abilities and self-awareness.

ANGELITE

Sweet, gentle, soft vibrations. Connects you to angelic healing, guidance, and frequencies, and enables you to see and communicate with angelic beings more clearly. Helps to quiet the mind and soothes anxiety.

AMAZONITE

Clears the pathway between the heart chakra and the throat chakra so that you're able to hear and honor your truth. Great for boundary issues, self-knowledge, open and honest communication, asking for what you want, and expressing your feelings and needs.

APACHE TEAR

Gentle healing from grief and loss, and recovery from shock. Soothing for the child within during times of dramatic change and great insecurity. Helps you face the fear of the unknown, both within and without.

AMETHYST

Raises your vibration, shifts negative thought patterns and habits, cools anger, calms anxiety, increases intuition, and shields against lower or harmful energy. Helps with sleep disorders and nightmares.

APATITE, BLUE

Empowers, amplifies, and directs vocal forms of manifestation. Reduces appetite, helps you feel secure in social situations, slows the aging process. Improves overall sense of well-being, fulfillment, and self-worth.

APOPHYLLITE

Helps you evolve into higher states of being and frees you from ego-based desires and attachments. Opens the crown chakra to receive higher guidance, channel divine light, and connect with ascended masters.

ARAGONITE STAR CLUSTER

High-frequency vibrations of Christ Consciousness, awareness, faith, fidelity, and leadership. Deeply healing for physical and emotional wounds. Improves feelings of confidence and self-worth.

AQUA AURA QUARTZ

Quartz altered by metallic vapors. Shields the aura against psychic attack. Increases feelings of conviction and courage; supports you in empowered communication and self-expression. Sparks the imagination and feelings of joy.

AVENTURINE, GREEN

Balances the heart chakra, increases vitality, attracts abundance, helps you feel more willing to receive. Improves overall health, especially cardiovascular and respiratory health.

AQUAMARINE

A stone of courage, grace, depth, willingness, authenticity, compassionate communication, articulation, calm, and Goddess energy. Cooling and soothing for the nervous system and emotions. Reduces inflammation, and promotes healing of ear, nose, and throat ailments.

AVENTURINE, PINK

Helps you feel more beautiful, desirable, and confident in your own skin. Makes your vibration more magnetic and attractive to others. Increases feelings of fun, playfulness, excitement, and flirtation.

AZURITE

Opens, restores, and strengthens the third eye chakra. Promotes psychic ability and clairvoyance. Frees you from limited thinking, improves the creative-thinking process. Good for headaches and eyestrain.

CALCITE, BLUE

Calming, soothing, relaxing energy. Helps balance emotions, calms overactive thinking, and soothes feelings of being too wired to relax or sleep. Good for sore throats, coughing, and respiratory illnesses. Gentle enough for children and pets.

BLOODSTONE

Grounding, balancing for the sacral chakra, mood swings, and hormonal balance. Accelerates recovery; helps with blood disorders and muscle, bone, and tissue healing; attracts abundance; increases one's ability to manage the everyday business of life.

CALCITE, CLEAR

Gently clears the crown chakra of any blockage, allowing for more divine light to flow through the body in support of spiritual healing and growth. Helpful for people who feel stuck or lost on their life path or purpose.

BLUE LACE AGATE

Energy flows from this crystal like smooth, cooling water. Calmly brings you back into focus and keeps you from feeling stressed, frazzled, or spun-out. Cools tempers, helps you to think more rationally, and reduces inflammation in the physical body. Gentle energy for children and pets.

CALCITE, GREEN

Refreshing and mildly invigorating energy that improves circulation and overall health, clears energy blocks in the heart chakra, and promotes respiratory health. Helps you feel more joy and express more gratitude.

CALCITE, HONEY
Helps you navigate through times of transition with grace and ease, letting go of what no longer serves you, changing, and moving on. Balancing for the solar plexus, healing for digestive disorders and inflammation.

CALCITE, ORANGE
Gentle restorative and revitalizing energy. Helps improve the flow of chi, creativity, and sensuality. Clears blocked energy in the sacral chakra, improves digestion, and strengthens the immune system. Excellent for hangovers and the flu.

CALCITE, MANGANO
Gentle, sweet, and soft vibrations. Therapeutic for loss and grief. Helps the child within heal and feel safe. Good for healing in cases of childhood trauma, violent crime, and deep self-loathing. Gentle enough for children and pets.

CALCITE, RED
Soothing yet replenishing energy that helps remedy feelings of burnout, exhaustion, and depletion. Helps to detoxify the system, improve circulation, clear blocked energy from the root chakra, and provide grounding, sustaining energy.

CALCITE, OPTICAL
Clear, rhomboid-shaped calcite. Excellent for visualization, manifestation, and shifting perspective. Therapeutic for excessive or overworked third eye chakras, headaches, and eyestrain.

CARNELIAN
Passionate, fiery, determined energy. Excellent for creative and artistic endeavors, performers, writers, and public speakers. Helps with empowerment and boundary issues, modifies destructive impulses, and increases feelings of confidence and self-worth. Boosts the libido.

CELESTITE

High-vibration crystal that improves your access to divine wisdom. Strengthens your connection to higher realms and beings, intensifies psychic phenomena and spiritual experience. Reduces pain and inflammation, and accelerates healing. Excellent for headaches.

CHRYSOCOLLA

Calming, nurturing energy. Enhances psychic abilities and intuition. Alleviates feelings of anxiety and dread, replenishes the adrenal system, and helps you feel and experience more compassion. Divine feminine energy.

CHIASTOLITE

Powerfully enhances psychic and spiritual abilities so that you can transcend everyday human experience to interact with trans-dimensional guides, beings, and spirits, and access ancient knowledge and divine wisdom. Strengthens your sense of self-sovereignty.

CHRYSOPRASE

Helps you feel more secure; reduces anxiety and feelings of social awkwardness. Encourages you to have more compassion for yourself and others. Restorative for empaths who feel drained of energy. Boosts creativity.

CHRYSANTHEMUM STONE

Clay-based stone of goodwill, good fortune, optimism, and abundance. Regular exposure to its energy draws luck, wealth, and happy circumstances into your experience. Shifts your mood and outlook from negative to positive.

CINNABAR QUARTZ

Cinnabar formed or encased in clear quartz. Powerfully attracts wealth, prosperity, property, abundance, and money. Strengthens feelings of personal power, capability, will, and ambition. Major energy boost for creative ideas and flow.

CITRINE

Energizing, brightens your mood, attracts prosperity, boosts confidence, increases creativity, and strengthens your immune system. It is a grounding crystal of optimism and mental stability, and it harmonizes with the three lower chakras and the third eye simultaneously.

EPIDOTE

Empowers the process of manifestation, amplifying its power and rapidly accelerating its results. Helps you to feel more confident in being able to co-create a more pleasant reality and have greater faith in your personal power.

DANBURITE

High-vibration crystal that rapidly expands the crown chakra, allowing you to experience higher realms, divine beings, and transcendence, and access the Akashic records with greater ease. Amplifies healing energy, prayers, and intentions.

EUDIALYTE

Grounding of heart energy in the root chakra, which supports you in identifying and successfully pursuing your dreams and life purpose. Helps you achieve your highest potential in this lifetime and attract romantic partnership.

EMERALD

Evolved heart energy. Helps you tap into your heart's fuller potential in terms of love, kindness, compassion, gratitude, and joy. A stone that attracts wealth and abundance. Healing for the heart and respiratory tract.

FIRE AGATE

Divine masculine energy. Good for strength, virility, creativity, passion, and fortitude. Excellent for boundary and empowerment issues, courage, inspiration, leadership, and grounding.

FLUORITE

A higher-mind stone. Activates, enhances, and increases all cognitive functions, including learning and memory. Healing for ADHD, schizophrenia, bipolar disorder, and learning disorders. Helps conceal and protect the aura from psychic attack and harmful entities.

HEALER'S GOLD

Enlightened, empowered, benevolent energy that is healing for all systems (physical, emotional, mental, spiritual, and the aura). Repels lower, harmful frequencies; increases your ability to channel healing energy and divine guidance.

FUSCHITE

Aligns our emotional selves with our physical reality, so that we are able to manage tasks, obligations, stressors, and needs without unnecessary emotional attachment, upset, or feelings of overwhelm. Helps us to shift our patterns of behavior from reactionary to responsive.

HEMATITE

Powerful grounding energy, increases vitality, stamina, strength, determination, chi, and accelerates the body's natural healing process. Helps you break the chains of addiction, bad habits, harmful behaviors, and past-life vows. Firmly anchors you in the body, the present, and the physical (material) plane.

GARNET (ALMANDINE)

Passionate, sexy, creative, sensual energy that increases your ability to feel pleasure and attract love and material prosperity. Helps you experience more inspiration, joy, desire, and motivation. Good for fertility and empowerment.

HERKIMER DIAMOND

High-vibration quartz that increases flow of chi and opens the third eye and the crown chakras. Powerfully heightens intuition, lucidity, and prophetic dream states. Promotes visionary and psychic abilities.

HIDDENITE (GREEN KUNZITE)

Attracts good luck and fortune, and puts you in the positive flow of synchronicity. Powerful vibrations of joy, optimism, goodwill, ease, happiness, and fulfillment.

JASPER, MOOKAITE

Helps you to relax and surrender to the natural flow and rhythms of the Earth and of your body. Improves sleep patterns, the ability to adjust to lifestyle and climate changes, and feelings of being grounded and connected to the Earth.

INFINITE

Heals and restores a damaged or depleted aura. Increases vitality and the flow of chi. Heightens your psychic senses and tunes them to the vibration of nature spirits, faeries, and ghosts.

JASPER, OCEAN

Soothing, uplifting, and restorative energy that helps you take a mental break when you're experiencing stress or work overload. Replenishing for the adrenal system and calming for the nervous system. Helps you feel happier and more at ease in social situations.

JADE (JADEITE)

A crystal of spiritual and personal mastery. Attracts good fortune, luck, prosperity, and material wealth. Supports spiritual growth, and brings divine help, guidance, and intervention in times of great need.

JASPER, RED

Courage, discipline, determination, endurance, stamina, and steady growth. Supports you through times of challenge, turbulence, and change. Keeps you feeling steady and able to move forward. Grounding, accelerates healing, and replenishes your energy field.

JASPER, YELLOW

Helps you temper control issues, workaholism, fear, and negative outlooks. Helps you bring a slower, steadier, more nurturing pace to your life. Increases feelings of overall well-being and fulfillment.

KYANITE, BLUE

Improves the ability to think, articulate ideas, communicate effectively, and recall information. Offers powerful protection from psychic attack. Strengthens intuition and your ability to understand divine guidance. Good for throat illnesses.

JET

Absorbs and grounds lower, harmful, and imbalanced energy. Safe to use on unborn babies, pets, plants, and children. Reduces feelings of stress and overwhelm. Helps the body detox.

LABRADORITE

Energy that encourages a transcendent or hypnotic state to plumb inner and cosmic mysteries. Helps with personal transformation and protects against psychic attack. Boosts your ability to access and recall arcane knowledge.

KUNZITE, PINK

Fills your heart with feelings of divine love and compassion, and strengthens your connection to Christ consciousness and your Higher Self. Helps you to overcome fear and recover from trauma, abuse, and PTSD.

LEPIDOLITE

Calming, soothing energy that has a quieting effect on the mind and the emotions. Excellent for sleeplessness and sleep disorders. Gently opens the third eye chakra when it's being blocked by fear and resistance. Helps to relieve coughs, pain, and anxiety.

LITHIUM QUARTZ

Rapid relief from anxiety, overwhelm, panic attacks, and moments of intense fear or insecurity. Soothing, warming, expansive heart energy that floods the system with loving vibrations and an overall sense of well-being. Relieves coughs.

MOONSTONE

Gentle, forgiving, intuitive, divine feminine energy. Helps you become more receptive to divine guidance and creative inspiration. Softens aggressive behavior. Protects you while in dream states and on vision quests.

MALACHITE

Powerful healing accelerator, both physically and emotionally. Brings repressed emotions to the surface to be released, clears blocked chakras, and is restorative for empaths by dissolving absorbed external energy within the system.

MOSS AGATE

Resonates powerfully with the natural kingdom, harmonizes with plant energy and green medicine. Attracts abundance, increases vitality, improves overall health and well-being.

MOLDAVITE

Accelerates the process of transformation, stimulates transdimensional experience, psychic abilities, spiritual awakening, and expansion. Supports you in achieving your highest potential. Can be overwhelming to the system and disrupt sleep patterns if used at night.

NUUMMITE

A stone of self-mastery, personal power, divine knowledge, and inner mystery. Empowering for mystics, spiritual healers, and psychics. Heightens psychic ability and spiritual experience. Resonates on a soul level.

OBSIDIAN, BLACK

Brings repressed or denied parts of yourself to the surface of your awareness so that they can be healed, reintegrated, or released. Shields you from witchcraft, psychic attack, and harmful entities. Excellent for shadow self work.

ONYX

Grounding, energizing, and motivating energy that improves focus, determination, and your ability to manage, delegate, and organize efficiently. Can be draining if worn for long periods.

OBSIDIAN, RAINBOW

Helps you to process heightened emotions and abrupt change, and assimilate new information. Soothing and grounding. Cloaks and shields the aura from psychic attack and psychic debris.

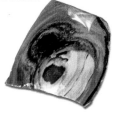

OPAL, PINK

Mellow, pleasant, and joyful energy that uplifts the spirit and helps you achieve and maintain a calm, optimistic, and open state of mind. Soothing and healing for the emotions.

OBSIDIAN, SNOWFLAKE

Grounds light in the body and spiritual experience in the physical; supports you in following divine guidance in your everyday life. Improves your ability to have faith and feel the presence of God or Source. Gently retrieves memories, including those of past lives.

PIETERSITE

Aligns your intuition with your will so that you're better able to trust, honor, and follow your own inner truth and guidance. Fine-tunes all forms of psychic ability, particularly clairsentience. Stirs up repressed or unacknowledged feelings and ignored intuitive guidance, and releases pent up frustrations.

PYRITE

Masculine, extroverted, yang, aggressive energy that helps you thrive, push through obstacles, and succeed. Boosts ambition, energy, and will; fires up the metabolism and aids digestion. Attracts money, wealth, and prosperity, and is excellent for manifestation. Grounding. Good for virility.

QUARTZ, ROSE

Love in a crystal. Soothing, nurturing, supportive, loving energy. Healing for the heart chakra and emotional wounds, recovery from shock, grief, loss, or trauma. Increases feelings of self-worth and self-love.

QUARTZ, CLEAR

Magnifies, amplifies, directs, intensifies, and channels energy. Can be used for any purpose, provided it's applied with clearly defined intentions. When combined or placed with other crystals, it will amplify and purify their energy and will recharge depleted crystals.

QUARTZ, RUTILATED (GOLD, SILVER, COPPER)

Quartz with gold-, copper-, or silver-colored strands of rutile. Increases energy, self-awareness, intuition, and connection to Spirit. Accelerates healing. Channels divine masculine, feminine, and angelic frequencies.

QUARTZ, ELESTIAL

High-vibration crystal that grounds spiritual and divine light in the body. Connects you to higher realms and angelic beings for guidance and to channel healing energy. Clears the aura of karmic and psychic debris. Helps foster greater soul-level alignment and awareness.

QUARTZ, SMOKY

Grounding, stabilizing, purifying energy. Helps eliminate stress and its effects on the system. Clears the aura of attachments and debris. Helps to detoxify the body.

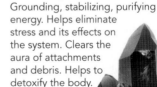

RHODOCHROSITE

Slowly and gently brings repressed emotions or memories to the surface of your awareness so that they can be healed, integrated, or released. Excellent for use in healing from trauma, sexual abuse, heartbreak, and loss. Attracts love, increases feelings of passion and resilience.

RUBY

Good for leadership, success, wealth, self-sovereignty, healthy boundaries, communication, empowerment, and determination. Increases the flow of passion, sensuality, pleasure, desire, creativity, and vitality through the system. Good for fertility. Attracts wealth. Grounding.

RHODONITE

Grounds you in your heart center, which helps you to make choices from a place of love. Boosts feelings of courage, especially when it comes to love. Helps to detoxify the system, primarily the liver. Supports you in pursuing your dreams and achieving your goals. Attract love.

RUBY IN FUSCHITE

Helps to bring you back to a state of calm, centered balance after moments of conflict, confrontation, shock, or high stress. Highly restorative energy for the emotional body.

RUBELLITE (RED TOURMALINE)

Opens, expands, and strengthens the heart chakra. Helps you feel more courage and compassion. Attracts romantic love. Improves your ability to experience divine love. Helps with the pursuit of your life purpose.

SAPPHIRE, BLUE

Improves all cognitive functions. Increases your ability to organize, troubleshoot, plan, strategize, communicate, and function at a higher level of efficiency. An antidote for overwhelming feelings, scattered attention, and bafflement.

SCOLECITE

High-vibration energy that helps you to harmonize and balance aspects of your radiant and shadow self, open yourself to the divine flow of healing energy, and surrender to divine timing and process. Improves feelings of trust and faith in God or the Universe.

SHIVA LINGAM

Balances masculine and feminine energy, increases vitality, intuition, and mindfulness. Grounding. Promotes fertility and virility. Improves feelings of strength, stamina, and power.

SELENITE

Dissolves energy blocks, cords, and psychic debris. Expands the crown chakra to receive divine guidance and access higher realms and beings of consciousness. Purifies energy. Relieves coughs, pain, inflammation, and tension, and promotes a feeling of calm and serenity.

SODALITE

Promotes self-awareness and helps you recognize patterns of behavior and self-limiting beliefs, identify authentic soul-based desires, and pinpoint inner workings. Increases cognitive functions. Improves intuitive abilities.

SEPTARIAN

A stone of humility, kindness, compassion, and grace. Enables you to see beyond your own needs and your own story to consider those of others. Helps you evolve into higher states of being and mindfulness.

SPIRIT QUARTZ (AKA CACTUS OR FAIRY QUARTZ)

Shields the aura and removes psychic debris. Protects against psychic attack and entity attachments. Revitalizes chi and dissolves blocked energy. Improves your ability to see and communicate with the faeries.

STAUROLITE

Enhances clairvoyance so that you can see through the veils of time, space, and dimension. Improves your ability to see, sense, and/or communicate with the faeries, plant spirits, and ghosts. Protects against malevolent energy and intentions.

TEKTITE

Helps you to cope with fear, frees you from a poverty mentality, limited thinking, and feelings of hopelessness. Increases the flow of chi from the crown chakra to the root, improving vitality and enabling you to live with greater divine purpose. High, energizing, fast vibrations.

SUGILITE

Offers powerful physical and emotional healing. Reduces feelings of fear and anxiety. Helps you to experience higher forms of consciousness and divine communication. Opens the third eye and expands the heart chakra.

TIGER EYE

Grounding, balancing, and centering energy. Helps with mood swings, insecurity, adaptability, stamina, and conviction of purpose. Increases primal instincts, intuition, and clairsentient abilities. Protective. Attracts prosperity and good fortune. Excellent for boundary issues.

SUNSTONE

Bright, divine masculine, empowering energy. Excellent for helping you to affirm and maintain healthy boundaries and feel a greater sense of personal power. Relieves feelings of apathy and stagnation. Optimism.

TIGER EYE, BLUE

Grounds the intuitive energy of the third eye chakra in the physical energy of the root chakra so that you can follow intuitive guidance more easily. Improves your ability to network and puts you in positive synchronous flow with divine intervention and timing.

TIGER IRON

Combination of tiger eye, hematite, and red jasper. Stealth, strength, and determination. Empowering, invigorating, grounding yang energy. Increases the flow of chi and circulation. Helps the body to rebuild and heal tissues, and accelerates cellular regeneration.

TOURMALINE QUARTZ

Clear quartz with black tourmaline inclusions. Purifies energy; clears auric psychic debris, blocked crown, and third eye chakras; alleviates congestion; and increases the flow of chi in ailing parts of the body.

TOPAZ, CLEAR

Accelerates the results of manifestation and visualization work. Helps you to picture things in your mind and visualize them more clearly. Improves recall and clairvoyance.

TOURMALINE, WATERMELON

Expands the heart chakra, increases feelings of self-love, passion for life, and courage, and helps cultivate greater feelings of warmth and compassion. Healing for grief, trauma, and bitterness. Attracts romantic love.

TOURMALINE, BLACK

Purifying, protective energy that helps to neutralize imbalances. Shields the aura from lower frequencies and etheric pathogens. Reduces pain and inflammation. Balances the emotions.

UNAKITE

Healing energy for the cardiovascular system and the spleen. Balances the emotions and our energy between spiritual and material concerns. Helps you to heal or replace bad habits and dependencies with healthier choices and options.